Vanishing Japan

Vanishing Japan

Elizabeth Kiritani

Japan

Traditions, Crafts, & Culture

Foreword by
Donald Richie

Illustrations by Itsuo Kiritani

Charles E. Tuttle Company
Rutland, Vermont & Tokyo, Japan

Much of the material in this book appeared in different form as a series of articles in the *Mainichi Daily News*, 1988–93. All twentieth-century Japanese names are in Western order; all earlier names are in traditional order, surname first.

During the period 1988–93 the exchange rate for Japanese yen was approximately 120 Japanese yen to the U.S. dollar.

Published by the Charles E. Tuttle Company, Inc.
of Rutland, Vermont & Tokyo, Japan
with editorial offices at
2-6 Suido 1-chome, Bunkyo-ku, Tokyo 112

© 1995 by Charles E. Tuttle Publishing Co., Inc.

LCC Card No. 95-60448
ISBN 0-8048-1967-X

First edition, 1995

Printed in Japan

Contents

Foreword   *by* Donald Richie 7

1 · On the Street
    Publicity Bands   *Chindonya*   14
    Candy Animals   *Amezaiku*   18
    Picture Theater   *Kamishibai*   22
    Potato Vendors   *Yakiimoya*   26
    Pipe Cleaners   *Raoya*   30
    Shoe Shiners   *Kutsumigaki*   34

2 · Housing and Interiors
    Natural Tatami   *Tatami*   40
    Interior Woodworkers   *Tateguya*   44
    Bamboo Blinds   *Sudare*   48
    Tile Roofs   *Kawara*   52
    Thatched Roofs   *Kayabuki Yane*   56
    Wooden Apartments   *Nagaya*   59

3 · Artisans and Crafts
    Clogs   *Geta*   64
    The Fire Brigade   *Hikeshi*   68
    Perfection of Skill   *Kijishi*   72
    Japanese Umbrellas   *Wagasa*   76
    Cotton Kimono   *Yukata*   80
    Edo-Style Joiners   *Edo Sashimono*   84
    Portable-Shrine Maker   *Miyashi*   88
    Woodblock Prints   *Ukiyoe*   92
    Name Stickers   *Senjafuda*   96

Edo Taste	*Kokan Nosatsu*	100
Paper Mounters	*Hyogushi*	104
Local Laborers	*Tobishoku*	108
Handmade Paper	*Washi*	112
Votive Plaques	*Ema*	116

4 · Festivals and Events

Spaced Out at Ueno	*Hanami*	122
Glory in the Flower	*Asagao Ichi*	126
Dancing in the Street	*Bon Odori*	130
Raking in the Money	*Otorisama*	134

5 · Seasonal Customs

Seasonal Markers	*Kisetsukan*	140
Natural Ice	*Tennengori*	144
Fire Watches	*Hi no Yojin*	148
Homemade Osechi Ryori	*Osechi Ryori*	152
Dreams of Revenge	*Hatsuyume*	156
New Year's Fun	*Hanetsuki*	160

6 · Daily Life

The Public Bath	*Sento*	166
Bathhouse Art	*Sento Haikeiga*	170
Cloth Wrapping	*Furoshiki*	174
Tangible Money	*Genkin*	178
Pawn Shops	*Shichiya*	182
Japanese Inns	*Ryokan*	186
Repairs	*Benriya*	190

7 · Entertainment

Geisha	*Geisha*	196
Kabuki Applause	*Kakegoe*	200
Shinto Juggling	*Daikagura*	204
Old Toys	*Dagashiya*	208

Index of Japanese Terms	213

Foreword

Donald Richie

Old Japan is vanishing. Traditional homes are being torn down, the public baths are closing; children no longer hopscotch among their chalked lozenges, their parents no longer sit on the stoop in the evening cool; the kimono has all but vanished, and tatami-mat rooms are no longer found in the newer apartments: even the food—such traditional fare as *kiji donburi* (pheasant over rice—deliciously faked, really chicken) and *hayashi raisu* (an Edwardian favorite, hashed rice)—must now be searched for. And in the place of all of this: the home shower, the chair and table, the TV set, and victuals known as finger-licking-good from the local corner shop.

So what else is new? Things come and go—change is the essence. This is something everyone knows, and most remark upon. The Japanese certainly know it, perhaps even better than some because the fact has been so publicly pondered and regretting it has become so institutionalized.

"The world of dew is, yes, a world of dew, but even so . . ." famously remarked Kobayashi Issa in 1819—as here translated by Sato Hiroaki. Transient, ephemeral, evanescent, our world vanishes before our eyes. This we know, can perhaps appreciate, can maybe celebrate, yet even so . . .

Even so, there is nostalgia and regret at the passing of things. There is the sadness of this knowledge of the impermanence of the only world we know and there is sorrow at the death of so much which is true and beautiful.

Our sentiment is so universal that we can only question its power to continue to move us as it does, and to wonder why this feeling should be so particularly poignant in regard to Japan.

Well, one of the reasons for this poignancy is that what we call old Japan is a product nowhere else duplicated. Old Europe and old America share much. The passing is sad perhaps but then one can still find pockets of the past in the Dolomites or the Ozarks and they resemble each other more than they don't.

But Japan, a distant archipelago which cut itself off from the world for centuries and had over the years evolved its own peculiar culture—there is no place else like this. And so when its various products—the traditional ryokan, older ways of counting and measuring, the tatami mat—slowly disappear, we are aware that we will never see them again. The poignancy is strongly felt because it is permanent. All of the pockets of the past are turned inside out.

Another reason for the poignancy is that the rate of change is here so accelerated. Japan is more ripe for change than other countries. Long a poor nation, it (or more properly speaking, its government and the resulting establishment) is now rich. Hence development, that friend to change, is rampant.

Mountains, forests, rivers, the shoreline itself—all are developed, which means drastically warped from their traditional shapes. Towns and cities get developed too, and if parts can no longer pay their way (the public baths, the old-style entertainments such as the *yose*, the *kamishibai* children's theater) then they disappear. Since change is expensive, old Japan could not formerly afford it. Now it can and there is a big backlog of true and beautiful things to be gotten rid of.

Also—a reason for the acceleration—Japan now has more people in it than ever before. This means less space. Old-time spreading out—whether in public parks or private houses—has become much more expensive. More efficient housing, more efficient methods of feeding, more efficient entertainment—all of this means enormous change. Brand-new products must be consumed in ever larger doses to spur an economy whose only consideration is its own steady growth. New products are welcomed everywhere in the world—if the hype is right—but only in Japan is the *shin hatsubai* (newly available) so ubiquitous as to be a national institution.

Added to this is a certain fecklessness, long visible and celebrated from the Edo era—it even had a name, *iki*—which finds in the changing fashions and the latest modes a gratification not unknown in other countries but seldom elsewhere found in such a lavishly concentrated form. Fads and fancies follow each other in an endless parade across the tube, the screen, and onto the streets. All of these are fittingly expensive and all are dependent only upon naked novelty.

Finally—another reason for Japan's particularly poignant reaction to change—is that it is acknowledged ("a world of dew") in the same breath as it is regretted ("but even so"). Though there are resigned repetitions of that national slogan, *shikata ga nai* (can't be helped), there is at the same time an acknowledged sadness, a public admission of the essentially tragic nature of life.

The officially optimistic West ("no use crying over spilt milk") has never understood this. Things over there always change for the better, in the long run, for the most people—and it is only the romantics at best, the old fogies at worst, who would think otherwise.

Japan is only cautiously optimistic. It seems from these shores that the mildly pessimistic might in the long run, for the most people, turn out to be the more accurate. Hence, hundreds of years ago, a name was given this benign sense of tragedy wherein dissolution was acknowledge, accepted, and to an extent even celebrated.

The name is *mono no aware*, a tangled term with a disputed etymology which nonetheless illuminates Japanese art and continues to lighten Japanese life. There are various interpretations. It has been compared to the Western *lacrimae rarum* as well as the universal stream of Heraclitus. Regarding vanishing Japan, however, a more homely illustration might be: Look into the mirror and regard one more wrinkle, one more gray hair. The proper *mono no aware* attitude is not to call up for an appointment at the beauty parlor but to gaze, find things going as they must and therefore should and, if possible, smile. This is *mono no aware* in action. And it is a term salient to the Japanese identity.

Around 1332, aesthetic recluse Yoshida Kenko, noting all the change around him, wrote that: "The most precious thing in life is its uncertainty." And in quoting this Donald Keene noted that indeed this is "the most distinctively Japanese aesthetic ideal—perishability."

Perishability as an ideal is not a notion familiar to nor congenial with the West. Over there, the way is to decry the change and then go ahead and embrace it. Over here, in Japan, the way is to embrace the necessity of the change itself.

Let us then, in old Japanese fashion, accept (*shikata ga nai*) necessary change. But in celebrating our very transience let us also remember. We should, as did Kenko, write about what has passed, make lists, catalogues, and celebrate what was with the same voice that we celebrate the need, even the virtue, of its passing.

This is what Elizabeth Kiritani has done. Here quite long enough to have seen massive change, she has compiled descriptions of this vanishing Japan—and Itsuo Kiritani has deftly sketched the buildings, the objects, the very people, before they disappear. In so doing they have both rendered the past alive.

One of the reasons they can do this is that they live in one of the last stands of old Tokyo. This is the neighborhood of Yanaka, only a fifteen-minute subway ride from the Ginza, but a warren of narrow streets, temples, stands of bamboo, bathhouses, mom-and-pop stores—some of the sights of which you can see in the illustrations in this book.

I live in Yanaka too, just up the street from the old Edo-style house where the Kiritanis live. And as I sit here, following my brush, as the old essayists say, a cool summer breeze wanders into my room, bringing with it the faint scent of lotus and the rich smell of mud, for just over that ridge of trees is Shinobazu Pond, the principal ornament of Ueno Park.

That it is still there, cool in the summer and home to hundreds of water birds, is due to Elizabeth and her neighbors. She has been socially useful and politically practical in joining (and creating) groups of concerned citizens who fight against avoidable and damaging changes which continue to threaten. Shinobazu has for the time being been saved from the developers who want a parking lot instead of a pond. She and her friends marched on the officials of Taito Ward and demanded that the pond remain. This time the developers backed down, but this eight-year-old battle still goes on.

Combining then a regard for the past with a critical eye to the future, Elizabeth Kiritani has—like Kenko before her—limned the vanishing with precision, with care, and with love. So long as her work remains, old Japan will not have vanished entirely.

Summer, 1994
Tokyo

On the Street

Publicity Bands

If you happen upon three or four people dressed outlandishly and dancing down the street banging on drums and tinny things,

sparkling as they twirl and shout, chances are that you have run across the *chindonya*. Skipping and dancing, they disappear down an alley only to re-emerge from another, the leader clanging his metal gong while making official-sounding announcements, a saxophonist at the rear. No, it's not the Mad Hatter's tea party gone berserk, but the last of a long tradition of street advertising.

Chindon tradition dates back to the Meiji Era (1868–1912), when they were called *tozaiya* or *hiromeya*. In those times, *jinta*, or street musicians, who later accompanied silent films, performed the same type of street advertising. When the talkies started, these musicians, as well as a lot of itinerant actors and actresses, lost their jobs and many of them became *chindonya*. The name *chindonya*—which came into use during the early Showa Era (circa 1926)—comes from the sound of the leader's metal and leather drums which make a "chin" and "don" sound. Of course, in the old days there was less street noise and the *chindonya* were very loud and conspicuous.

The golden age of the *chindon* business was between 1946 and 1956, when work was plentiful and lucrative. Kinosuke Hanashima is the boss of a group that occasionally works in our neighborhood. His father and mother had been *chindonya* after the war and when his father died, he had to quit his job as a city worker to accompany his mother and help support their large family. His is a popular group: he has received four silver and at least ten bronze medals from the *chindon* association for their performances.

A group usually has seven members, of which up to four work at one time. This is so that at busy times the group can work two jobs by splitting up into one group of three and another of four. The one who heads the group as they proceed down the street is the *hatamochi* (or *hataodori*) who carries a flag and gives out leaflets. He or she is followed by the *oyakata*, the boss, who carries the *chindon* drums with their large paper umbrella propped up over them. The third in procession used to play the *shamisen*, but now is the *doramuya*, with one large drum, and the fourth is the *gakkiya*, or musician, who plays the saxophone, clarinet, or trumpet, in that order of popularity.

Costumes are determined by the *oyakata* and tend to be flamboyant. In Mr. Hanashima's group all (but the musician) wear *chonmage* (topknot) wigs, thick pancake makeup, and an eccentric combination of old Japanese clothing adorned with sequins. The musician is dressed like an old-time Westernized dandy: jacket, tie, and a rakish porkpie hat. The best groups are a mix of men and women—and most are made up of people whose roots are in the theater, music, or the arts.

Nowadays the advertising is mostly for pachinko parlors, store openings, and shopping area bargain sales. Sponsors are thinning out and Mr. Hanashima says that they work only about fifteen days a month. They make 15,000 yen apiece per day, so it costs 60,000 yen to engage them for a full day (10:30 A.M.–5:00 P.M.).

According to Mr. Hanashima, there are about forty groups in

Japan, twenty of which are in or around Tokyo. He says it's a pleasant job in that most members are artists of some sort, they are doing what they want to do, and there is no retirement age. An energetic sixty-one, he looks forward to continuing for as long as he can. The bad side is that there are fewer and fewer sponsors. Times are tight, so if you're thinking of a surprise for your next party, you may be able to get a bargain. If you ask, though, remember to call them *"chindon* men." Mr. Hanashima says that this is the most flattering term for them—a nickname coined at the time when the "sandwich man" was the rage.

About 120 shops make up northern Tokyo's Kyoseikai shopping area, which had commissioned the group for one day in late December. They started off down the main street, greeting shop owners gaily, and then disappeared down the back alleys of the neighborhood where they would regale potential customers for the rest of the day. I asked one of the greengrocers whether he thought that the *chindonya* would increase his sales. A dubious look crossed his face. "Hmmm, I wonder . . ." was all he said. Toshie Tanaka, proprietress of a shop that sells tea, was more positive. She explained that they hire this group twice a year, right before New Year and Obon. "They wander through the neighborhood and create an atmosphere conducive to buying," she explained. "People hear them and think there is something special going on that they don't want to miss. Besides, we enjoy having them here. It brightens up our day too, you know."

Candy Animals

You may get a peek at an *amezaiku* (candy artisan) this summer, if you're lucky. The remaining few are being hired for private parties, so running into one in the street is quite an event. But they still appear at some of the big festivals. Tokyo's top candy virtuoso, Ki Aoki, always has a stall at the Yasukuni Shrine for its Obon (July 13–16) and New Year (December 30–January 4) festivals.

I located him this year by the boisterous cluster of school girls in yellow backpacks and straw hats surrounding him. "Make a swan, make a koala," they shouted. As Mr. Aoki made the animals, he told jokes. One little girl was holding a large bag against her chest. "Moving, are ya?" he quipped. The kids tittered. "You'd better go home now (they are *en route* from school). Bring your mother or grandfather with you tonight and I'll show you some more." The old sales pitch.

But Mr. Aoki's best customers aren't kids. They're OLs (office ladies) in their twenties. "The kids have no time to come back. They're on schedules," he explains. According to his wife, prices haven't changed much over the years. They range from 300 yen for a simple rabbit (*usagi*) to 1,500 yen for a raccoon dog (*tanuki*) with the standard hat and accessories. Most of the items he crafts cost 500 yen.

A tradition said to have started in Osaka in the early 1800s, candy-animal making requires more skill than is apparent. Just preparing the candy is tricky. Glutinous rice (*mochi gome*) and potato powder are boiled carefully to a specific transparent doughy texture, and then hand pulled and kneaded. Contact with the air during this process produces the pure white color. It is then rolled into a huge ball and allowed to harden until ready for use.

Tadon (charcoal) in the box of the *amezaiku's* cart heats the large candy ball into a pliable mass. Animals must be formed quickly before the candy hardens—a rabbit, for instance, takes about thirty seconds. Dexterity, an artistic sense, and a lot of imagination are needed.

The challenge is to find an animal or bird that Mr. Aoki can't make. The last of the experienced *amezaiku* in Tokyo, he keeps up with comic and cartoon animals as well as regular bird and animal species. Doves, unicorns, Australian lizards, welcoming cats, and, most difficult of all, dragons are standard items. He scoops a wad of hot white candy in his hand, rolls it into a ball, and snips it here and there with razor-sharp tweezer-scissors to make his specialty: the intricate fanned wings of a crane.

Hooked around his middle finger and extending back over his forearms are his *tekko*. These decorative cloth coverings serve as sweat guards. The work is hot. During his thirty years of experience, Mr. Aoki has had a number of apprentices, but all quit before they had learned the trade. "The candy burns your hands. It's painful and hard to get used to." The miniature scissors are also dangerously sharp. Although lucrative private parties have sparked new interest in the occupation in Tokyo, the difficulty of the work has kept the number of *amezaiku* down to less than ten.

One thing Mr. Aoki won't make is a frog. Whenever he makes a frog it starts to rain. "*Ame* (rain) is not good for the *ame* (candy) business," he jokes.

A *hachimaki* (cloth headband) is twisted around Mr. Aoki's forehead and he's wearing a navy *happi* coat with a *donburi* in place of a shirt. This *donburi* is a short indigo apron with a large kangaroo pouch in front. You see it at all festivals. Mr. Aoki's pants are tight *momoshiki*, also festival garb. His lively wife, Eiko, his assistant for twenty years, is dressed in indigo as well. She cools the animals in front of a fan to set their shape before applying an assortment of red, yellow, and green colors.

"Many of the animals used to be blown like glass," she says, "but this was prohibited around 1973 for hygienic reasons. Now if you want to make a blown one, the customer must blow it himself or, as in Kansai, a rubber pump is used."

What do they taste like? I don't know. You buy one and see if you have the heart to eat it.

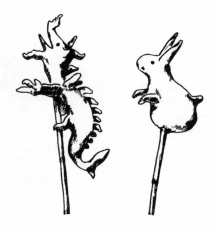

Picture Theater

When the *hyoshigi*, or wooden clappers, rang out, children knew which of the theater men had arrived. Each had his own rhythm that served as a calling card, one that children could understand. This was because many bicycle-riding theater men showed up at the same park or quiet street, and each man had to establish himself as a special story-teller in order to make a living.

The golden age of *kamishibai* (picture theater) was right after the war when many people were out of work. At this time there were over 3,000 *kamishibai* in Tokyo alone. It was a job that required little capital to pursue—a bicycle, a drum, and a frame for the theater with drawers under it for candy. The hand-painted pictures that were displayed in the frame were rented by the month. The trick was having the kind of candy kids liked and being able to spin a yarn in an engrossing way. Every day, just at the height of the drama, the play was stopped, to be continued in installments.

The storytelling itself wasn't so difficult because the rented pictures that were pulled one at a time from the theater frame had the story written on their backs. All the performer had to do was read. But the audience was discriminating. Voice and expression were important. The drum had to be used to good effect—rumbling ominously to indicate danger, accentuating the action, surprising the audience. And all this was only to attract the audience. The *kamishibai* man made his living from selling the candies that the kids ate while watching his show.

Ask any elderly Japanese about *kamishibai* and you are likely to get a nostalgic response. But the men performing it were living

precariously; they had no health or retirement insurance, and, of course, they had no income on rainy days. It was for this reason that so many of these men and their picture painters became Communists. They were struggling and needed organized help. Even today, the Communist link still exists. It was at a party given in honor of Seiji Asai's book about the history of labor unions and *kamishibai* that I first became aware of this. A Communist Party politician made a congratulatory speech, and after he disappeared there was a lot of discussion about Communism and the struggles of the past.

There were several *kamishibai* men at this party, as well as Koji Kada, one of the main painters for the theater. Misao Naito pulled out a harmonica and played for us, after which he gave a humorous speech. A natural performer, he was eager to entertain, and did so with ease. The others competed in their own ways—men in their seventies, all with that warm talkative quality peculiar to successful festival merchants.

A few weeks later, Mr. Naito gave his first performance in thirty years at the Katsushika Techno-Plaza. Mr. Naito's appeal was obvious from the start in his smile, his gruff voice, his ease and shine with the audience. But we were indoors, the children were used to TV, and a microphone was in full squeak. It was a complicated story, *Golden Bat*, about the war—one of the few original picture sets that had not been lost.

During the performance the adults recalled those afternoons when they had sat on the ground, chewed on candy, and puzzled over quizzes while watching this theater. It had been their sole entertainment after school—they had had no cram schools, no TV, no computer games. If they could bite a pink rice cracker into a certain animal figure, they would get a prize; if they could crack the quiz they would win free candy. Some thirty years had passed, but the parents at the Techno-Plaza were playing with the old toys and eating candy, enraptured. Their kids stood nearby with bored-looking expressions.

Today, there is still one *kamishibai* man working in Tokyo. He appears occasionally near the Nippori JR Station. He is worth searching for because he is the last chance to see the real thing. He works outside, regaling his audiences in the traditional way, without microphones, electric lights, or other modern paraphernalia.

Potato Vendors

Do you know the night *ramen* vendor's distinctive three-toned whistle? How about the knife sharpener's or the bamboo seller's special calls? Or the tofu man's whistle? They can still be heard in Tokyo's *shitamachi* (old, working-class neighborhoods). Certainly one call that everyone can recognize is the *yakiimo* man's. If you're lucky, you'll hear it coming from a cart pushed along the street and not from one of those trucks that fume up our environment. Who are these men who brave the cold to sell us those delicious potatoes? What do they do from late March to November when the season is over? Their life is not easy, and their tradition continues from centuries ago.

Monouri, or street vendors, were at work in the Heian Period (794–1185) although it wasn't until the Muromachi Period (fourteenth century) that they became a vital part of the economic system. They not only sold food, tools, toys, medicine, and small things for daily use, but some also bought used articles such as old clothes, umbrellas, and metal, and still others served as repairmen for knives, clogs, and the like. Some *monouri* specialized in seasonal goods such as decorations for the New Year, irises for Boy's Day, goldfish for summer, lanterns for Obon, and insects for children in the summer.

The life of the *monouri* was a hard one. During the Edo Period (1603–1868) selling became desperately competitive, and vendors began to don exotic costumes, use amusing and attention-getting calls, and even perform engaging antics in order to attract business.

The *tojiname uri*, for instance, who sold candies to children, wore

Chinese clothes and a Chinese hat. He played a flute and drum, and delighted his young audience with dancing whenever he made a sale. The *takarabune uri*, active until the mid-Meiji Era, sold prints of the Seven Lucky Gods (*shichifukujin*) that you see here and there every New Year. People slept with these prints under their pillows to induce a lucky dream for the year. *Soba* vendors hung *furin* (chimes) on the carriers worn on their backs and jangled their way along the narrow streets. It must have been a noisy city even without the help of motorcycles and loudspeakers.

Although *yakiimo* (baked sweet potatoes) were popular in the Edo Period, they were sold only in stores—probably due to fire laws. Only boiled and steamed potatoes were sold by the street vendors. Today, in *shitamachi*, *yakiimo* are baked in pebbles that are heated by a wood-burning stove in the bottom of a wooden cart. Once fully cooked (after about one hour), they are raked out of the pebbles and placed in the adjacent warming compartment until they are sold.

My favorite *yakiimo* man, Mr. Nagao, is from Aomori. I came to know him because of his call. A veteran *minyo* and *enka* (traditional Japanese styles of singing) performer, his call is a distinct and beautiful distraction among the confusion of everyday noise. He is one of twelve men who are under his *oyakata* (boss) in the Ueno area. He says there are about ten bosses in Tokyo now, and each is in charge of a certain area. Mr. Nagao has been working my street for twenty winters. He sleeps in a nearby six-mat room that he shares with two older *yakiimo* men in their seventies, also from the Tohoku district.

Mr. Nagao is a rice farmer. After the harvest at the end of October, he comes to Tokyo to work until the end of March while his rice paddies are under snow. He sells sweet potatoes from 10:00 A.M. until 9 or 10:00 P.M., six days a week. He cooks for himself in his small room and, occasionally, goes out for drinks and *karaoke* at a local bar. Being away from home and eating the limited menu that he cooks are the hardest parts of his job, he says.

Just as in the Edo Period, he must rent his cart (2,500 yen a month) and buy potatoes (9,000 yen per 40 kilograms) from his *oyakata*. Things are tight now. As recently as 1981, he sometimes sold 100 kilograms of potatoes per day, but now he is lucky if he sells 20. At about 600 yen per kilogram, this doesn't leave much to take home after rent, food, and expenses. His most frequent customers, he says, are middle-aged women, and the best time of day for business is 3:00 P.M. The tall, noiseproof new buildings and the popularity of Western-style candy have reduced his sales.

At the end of last year he wasn't sure whether it would be worth his while to come again this season. So, one day in late October when we heard his distinctive cry, we smiled, knowing he was back. Whether he'll be back again next year is another question. Have you had a *yakiimo* lately?

Pipe Cleaners

Tobacco made its way to Japan from America via the Portuguese and Spaniards at the end of the sixteenth century. It was extolled for its medicinal properties: "If a sick man tastes this smoke he is restored to glowing health," wrote Prince Toshihito in 1609. Times have changed for tobacco. And so have the ways of smoking it.

Cigars appear to have come first. The record is sketchy, but soon a long thin pipe called a *kiseru* became *de rigueur* for men and women of all strata in Japan, despite sporadic and futile government intervention.

Among other things, smoking was thought to help fix the black color that married women applied to their teeth, giving the *kiseru* allure as an odd sort of beauty aid. Shopkeepers smoked *kiseru* with flat mouthpieces that teeth could clamp down on to free hands for business; the samurai's was thin and elegant; the sumo wrestler's huge; the actor's distinctive and easily recognized. At one point some townspeople brandished heavy, studded *kiseru* called "squabble pipes" as substitutes for the swords they were not permitted to carry.

Materials for the bowl and mouthpiece of the *kiseru* included ceramics, stone, ivory, silver, and gold, but copper was the most prevalent. These ends were joined by a stem of bamboo. *Raoya*, the name for men who clean and refit the bamboo, bowl, and mouthpiece of *kiseru*, comes from the word for Laos, where this bamboo was originally from. *Kiseru* is a Cambodian word. Just why such a word came to be used for Japanese pipes remains unclear.

Tomeshiro Nakajima, like his father before him, has been servicing *kiseru* for forty-six years. If you visit Asakusa's Kannon Temple on a weekend, you may run into him, the very last *raoya*, or *kiseru* cleaner, in Japan.

He takes up a spot in front of the main gate of the temple, in an indigo coat and straw hat with a long *kiseru* pipe in hand, looking like something right out of the Edo Period. He'll be leaning on his stalwart bicycle whose sidecart forms a wooden store with glass windows protecting a row of antique *kiseru*. Inside also is a peculiar potbellied stove. A wooden shelf folds out to one side proffering less expensive *kiseru* and the pale *kiseru* tobacco to the hands of the masses. Some of this tobacco lies out in a bowl from which Mr. Nakajima fills and refills his long pipe. Different from cigarette or cigar tobacco, this *kizami* is chopped into fine hair-like strands.

The storecart has a roof from which three odd chimneys jut, gaily puffing out smoke. Two are whistles and the third serves as an outlet for the potbellied stove. This stove contains the charcoal upon which Mr. Nakajima lights his long *kiseru*. It also holds a compartment of boiled water to flush out clogged pipes. When a lever is pulled, steam whooshes out one or the other of the whistles making a high-pitched sound to announce his proximity or a soft lower sound to signal that he has stopped somewhere. In the past, regular customers would recognize his particular sound and run out to catch him.

These days, of course, there are not many people wanting their *kiseru* cleaned or bamboo refitted. That's not to say that people don't use *kiseru*, reassures Mr. Nakajima. It's just that they use cheaper ones which they can throw out once the geriatric symptoms of stenosis appear.

Until recently, Mr. Nakajima's business was almost exclusively repairing pipes. Drawers in his cart still burst with tools—long rods to push out black worms of tar, saws and knives to fit bamboo snugly to bowl and mouthpieces. His heyday was just before and after the war because when tobacco became scarce, real addicts didn't want to dilute it by smoking it with paper. Nowadays, it's a rare pipe he fixes. But he has a brisk business in cheap *kiseru* sales.

His customers vary, I saw as I watched him work one chilly March afternoon. Mr. Nakajima enjoys interaction with people, be they natives or foreigners. Language is no barrier. He finds a friendly way to communicate by offering a toke off his pipe to a curious foreigner, or by sharing reminiscences with a lingering elder. Wham, wham—he knocks the remnants out of the bowl of his pipe, smiling all the while with the brown teeth of a connoisseur. He puffs on Virginia Slims between pipes.

People come and go. Whenever one person stops to look, a whole swarm joins. An eager look flickered across one Middle Easterner's face when he saw the *kizami*. "Hashish?" he queried hopefully. "Try it and see," laughed back Mr. Nakajima in a jumble of English, Japanese, and gesticulation. A purchase. An elderly woman in kimono appeared. "My mother used one," she commented. "Not like these, but a smaller, thinner one which she wrapped in cloth before placing it in her obi." A purchase. The most surprising buyer, though, was a middle-aged man, wife and child in tow, who wandered over, glanced at the case of antique *kiseru*, and, with little more than a nod, bought the silver-tipped one for 20,000 yen. Mr. Nakajima concurs that business these days is pretty good.

Shoe Shiners

Fuyo Torimoto is crouched under her all-purpose umbrella from 10:00 A.M. to 6:00 P.M., as she has been for the past thirty-five years, along the main street of Sapporo between Odori Park and Odori Subway Station. Her business year extends from early May until late October, when the snow appears. Other than very rainy days, she is out there every day, patiently waiting and observing the comings and goings from street level, perched on her *zabuton* cushion, legs folded beneath her. She has seen a lot of changes in the last four decades, she says, especially in regard to her work on the streets.

She provides her own tools and equipment, which include the all-purpose rain and sun umbrella, twenty-eight colors of shoe polish, chair, foot stand, brushes, cloths, cleaning fluids, myriad paraphernalia including a small surrounding fence, her *zabuton*, leg warmer (in autumn), thermos, and so on. At night she stores it all in compact form in a parking lot around the corner. The price list leaning against her polish box reads: usual 300 yen, two colors 350 yen, white shoes 500 yen, golf shoes 600 yen, suede shoes 550 yen, boots 550 yen.

We were on our way to graphic designer Kenichi Kuriyagawa's opening

party at the Grand Hotel when my husband glanced down at my
tan high heels and scolded me for not taking better care of them.
"People in Japan polish their shoes," he grumbled, just as we were

passing Mrs. Torimoto's stall. Seizing the moment, I plunked myself down on the fold-out chair and gave her what must have been an unusual challenge: shoes that hadn't been polished in two whole years.

Ten minutes and 300 yen later the shoes had been transformed almost as if by magic and I had been entertained thoroughly by this vibrant, industrious seventy-five-year-old woman. It was no surprise to learn that she has a number of "steady customers"—mostly businessmen—who stop regularly to have a chat and polish three or four times a month, year after year. "Even though business is waning, it's a job that can really educate you in many ways," she said. "And it certainly is a whole lot better than staying home and watching TV."

Mrs. Torimoto has been a widow since the war and has had to struggle to bring up her daughter. Now she has two grandsons of whom she is proud, and she spends the money she makes from her shoe polishing on presents and things that she likes to buy for these kids.

In 1952 there were about 180 shoe shiners lining the main street from Sapporo Station to Susukino; today there are only 23. "One of the reasons, of course, is that shoe shining isn't a very appealing job for young people," she says. "They'd rather be doing something more active than sitting around and waiting for a pair of dirty shoes to show up. But this isn't by any means the whole reason," she adds.

"Take a look at the shoes people are wearing today," she shakes her head from side to side. "Just look at them! The high heels are all made out of vinyl. Cheap! You can't polish vinyl. People are no longer buying fine leather shoes. Some men still do, of course, but they are getting to be fewer and fewer. And you can't polish sneakers, either," she added.

These days she shines an average of seven or eight pairs of shoes a day: about 2,400 yen's worth. During the day when she isn't busy shining shoes and chatting to her customers, a fellow shiner often stops by to share some news or part of her lunch. Mrs. Torimoto is fortunate to have a place to live and enough money to live on. In her case, the business of shoe shining is more than just a paying job. It is a connection to the everyday world, a connection to other people, her polishes reflecting a life dedicated to hard work and endeavor.

Housing and Interiors

Natural Tatami

"Nyobo to tatami wa atarashii ho ga yoi" (wives and tatami are both best when new) is a comment on the delightful fresh smell of new tatami mats. This old saying may be obsolete on both counts. The modern bride's housekeeping and cooking skills have been reduced by the demands of the educational system. And with "modernization" and "improvements," the tatami of today may not be what it seems. In any case, whenever one conjures up a picture of Japan, tatami, along with kimono and cherry blossoms, invariably comes to mind. As section after section of Japan's cities are being rebuilt, what is happening to the ubiquitous tatami?

Tatami itself isn't vanishing, but perhaps the trade of making it is. Most new houses have only one tatami room, either the living room or guest room. But although today's homes have fewer tatami, the construction boom is stimulating a lot of business, making it difficult to determine the actual decline in use.

Tatami is composed of three separate parts—*toko*, *omote*, and *heri*—made by different artisans and assembled by "tatami makers" in their small shops. About 23,000 of these *tatamiya* remain, although the number is decreasing every year.

The *toko*, or base, is five centimeters thick and is, traditionally, made of pressed straw woven with linen threads (the woof). Machine woven since the Taisho Era (1912–26), *toko* lasts forty years or more. The longer the *wara* (straw) used, the higher quality the mat. Because rice-harvesting machines chop *wara* into short pieces that are unsuitable for tatami, Japan has been importing *wara* from Taiwan for over ten years now.

The *omote*, the thin visible surface, is made of *igusa* (rush), the majority of which is woven in Okayama, Hiroshima, Fukuoka, and Kumamoto. With traditional *wara toko*, the *omote* is used for three years, reversed for another two years, and then replaced.

The third part, the *heri*, is the border that once was silk, linen, or cotton, but is now mainly synthetic fabric. Unlike previously, today *heri* patterns and colors are freely chosen by the user. Rooms with a *tokonoma* (wall niche for displaying art or flowers), however, still frequently have a *mon* (crest) pattern on the *heri*.

Over the ages, tatami size was gradually standardized so completely that the number of mats a room can contain became a way of measuring its size. But the standards are relative: the size of tatami varies according to region. A twelve-mat room in Tokyo is considerably smaller than one in Kyoto.

During the Heian Period (794–1195), only court people used tatami. The color of the *heri* indicated the owner's rank. The higher the rank, the more mats they could pile up to elevate their sitting positions. It wasn't until the late 1600s that ordinary households had tatami. In terms of expense, today a tatami room costs roughly three times as much as a regular room to build.

Tatami has a practical side that, despite its higher price, ensures its continued use in Tokyo and similarly crowded cities. A tatami room can sleep many, whereas a room with beds can sleep only one or two. Tatami rooms can also be used for multiple purposes: in my home, our four-and-a-half-mat room serves as our dining room, living room, kitchen, guest room, and bedroom. How's that for economy?

Tatami is increasingly being made of plastic. According to Chojiro Shimizu, head of the National Federation of Tatami Unions, the majority of new tatami *toko* consists of a thin oil-based perforated plastic with thick Styrofoam beneath it. This innovation is promoted by construction companies due to lower cost (not necessarily for the customer), light weight (a new-type mat weighs less than five kilograms; real tatami can weigh up to thirty kilograms), and easy maintenance (no bugs; no need for airing).

The "breathing quality" of natural tatami, which absorbs as much as one cup of moisture per mat, is lost. Natural tatami also reduces noise, is good insulation, biodegradable, and not so hazardous during a fire. And for anyone sitting *seiza* style (on folded legs) for any length of time, there is a real difference in comfort.

What about the bugs or fleas that are occasionally attributed to tatami? According to Mr. Shimizu, new *toko* must be aged a full year before use to ensure bug-free mats. Once installed, traditional mats should be stacked outside, aired, and beaten twice a year. Mr. Shimizu added that the city of Tokyo encourages the use of plastic mats because the semiannual airing process produces four times the amount of trash on airing days. This strains the city clean-up services. I myself prefer the inconvenience of airing and pounding rather than having to put up with pain in my legs caused by the newer species. My husband Itsuo, who has to lug the thirty kilogram mats outdoors, may have a different opinion.

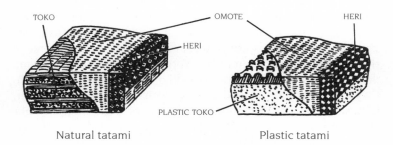

Natural tatami   Plastic tatami

Interior Woodworkers

The realm of the *tateguya* is architectural openings: windows, doors, and the like. Until the medieval ages their work was done by regular carpenters, but by the seventeenth century, the independent *tateguya* had come into being. At this time stores, brothels, and restaurants had increased the demand for fancy woodwork. Due to strict Edo anti-luxury regulations, though, the real *tategu* renaissance came after the Meiji Restoration (1868).

The advent of aluminum doors and windows pulled the rug out from under the Maejimas' traditional profession. After the war they had been too busy to relax, except for the months of January and February when cold and ice prevent them from working on lacquered wood. A major part of the lives of Masaji Maejima and his younger brother Yasuji has been dedicated to making *amado*, glass and shoji wooden frames, *itado*, and *ranma*, items which many are totally unfamiliar with today.

The *amado*, or rain shutter, dating from the sixteenth century, is a traditional type of wooden storm window—often hidden in a design panel on the outside of a house—that is slid closed during storms and at night for protection. Some modern homes use aluminum equivalents that slide out from aluminum sheds on either side of a window. The precursors of shoji, or translucent paper sliding screens, were *tsuitate* shoji: stand-up movable screens that were first used in temples to separate spaces in large rooms during the Nara Period (710–94). By the Heian Period (794–1185), they and other forms called *ita* shoji, which consisted of wooden frames with paper or cloth pasted on them; *akari* shoji, or light shoji, with paper or silk on a lattice; and *fusuma* shoji with two layers of paper had come into use. A*kari* shoji allowed diffused light to enter the home, and their soft moonlight inspired an orgy of poetic descriptions. This is the same type of shoji that is still used today, although current shoji are "plain Janes" when compared to the fancy pictorial lattice designs of the past. Sliding wooden doors, *itado*, are unique to Japan. Other countries that have used sliding doors have suspended them from above; none has run them from top and bottom as in Japan. *Ranma*, the fancy wooden partition designs hung from the ceilings between rooms, provided ventilation as well as decoration.

Masaji and Yasuji Maejima, both dressed in gray pants and jackets, work in a huge workshop beneath Masaji's second-story living quarters in Tsukishima, an old island community in Tokyo Bay. There are large machines along the periphery and one entire wall is hung with wooden-handled tools, the majority of which are planes of all sizes. An old potbellied stove squats near the doors, unused. Other than this, wooden shavings and stacks of spruce and other woods, the room is an open space. It's the end of March, a chilly rainy day. As the brothers talk in their mild, quiet tones, large puffs of breath evaporate in midair.

They are ambivalent about progress. The new machines are great—manual planing had been back-breaking. Yet, before, customers had made more special orders and were particular about the woods to be used. Many would come to select wood personally. Also, handmade products have a particular sheen that cannot be reproduced by machine. Now that most things are ordered by large construction companies and sizes are uniform, about half of their business involves working as wholesalers of factory-made units. Special orders are falling off, but there are more than enough orders for ready-made doors and windows. So their work is now easier and more lucrative.

A third-generation *tateguya*, Masaji was trained before the war from the age of fifteen and worked every day from morning to night except on the first and fifteenth of the month, his days off. After the war, their working time (previously about eleven hours a day) was stretched to fourteen hours because they were so busy. Even after aluminum windows first came into use in the early 1960s the Maejimas were constantly busy because the variety of door and window sizes required their custom services. But once measurements became standardized, special factories took over.

What about the fourth generation? Both Masaji and Yasuji smile bashfully. Of Masaji's three sons, one is a technician, one sells fish at Tsukiji, and the youngest works for Fuji-Xerox. Yasuji's son is a draftsman of government bonds. Shoulders are shrugged. There's a perfectly good business selling pre-made materials, but the skill and finesse of their profession are rarely called into practice these days. Both are adamant, though, that although changes in their business are fine by them, the old two-story wooden homes—the product of their traditional work—offer a far better lifestyle than that of the new buildings that are fast destroying the old neighborhood of Tsukishima.

Bamboo Blinds

Weathered *sudare* hanging outside the windows of traditional housing in Kyoto is quintessential Japan. During the summer season, even those of us in Tokyo can see them because their uses as mosquito netting and sunshades still linger in the back streets of Tokyo as well as in the countryside. *Sudare* have a long history. They're mentioned in the *Man'yoshu*, the eighth-century compilation of poetry. By Heian times, *sudare* (then called *misu*) had cloth edges and were used in the Imperial Court, shrines, and temples to divide spaces or provide shade. Their exclusive use by the nobility, however, ended because of their convenience as sunshades, bug screens, natural ventilators, mold preventers, and so on. They even had official use on the entertainment boats that plied the Sumida River during the Edo Period (1603–1868). Boats for commoners were required to have *sudare* rather than shoji panels to facilitate spot inspections during the periodic crackdowns on prostitution.

Before the war there had been 126 registered *sudare* makers in Tokyo. Now there are about 13, most of whom are using plastic materials or making modern blinds along with their traditional work. Good quality materials are harvested from the wild and include bamboo, bush clover, cattails, and various reeds. Due to urbanization, however, these natural materials are in short supply. *Sudare* cannot be hung from the aluminum frames of modern buildings, and air conditioning has taken over their primary function.

To find out more about *sudare*, I visited the Tanaka Seirenjo Company in Asakusa. The Tanaka family's business dates back to the Edo Period, and Kotaro, at twenty-eight, is the family's fifth-generation *sudare* maker. Three generations are now working together. Their shop's step-up interior has a clean, cool feel to it, perhaps from the butter-smooth wooden floor, perhaps from the bundles of reeds, rush, and bamboo of various browns and beiges that are stacked everywhere. Their two foot-operated, hand-fed machines that sew reeds together (formerly with pure silk, these days with a rayon-cotton blend) have been in use since the Taisho Era (1912–26). The wood-framed, glass walls are flung open and a calico cat on a homemade leash watches over the operations.

Kotaro's grandfather, Masao, has been in the business for sixty-four years. A lively eighty with a vigorous head of white hair and a

towel around his neck, he unrolls some thick bamboo *sudare* with large kanji cut into them and thinner reed blinds, very fine and just barely transparent. He's proud of their work. Material colors and sizes have been carefully matched and the beautiful patterns of bamboo joints that decorate some of the screens have been painstakingly arranged. Prices range from 500 yen for a coaster to about 200,000 yen for a *sudo*, a large wood-framed shoji panel fitted with bush clover instead of *washi*. His son, Yoshihiro, who has about thirty-five years of experience, explains that part of the problem these days is communication. In the past, *sudare* were sold by people who knew and talked about their wares. Such communication between buyer and seller no longer exists, so few people know about the various types of bamboo blinds available and their uses. For instance, *sudare* is not exclusively for summer use: some forms are hung on northern surfaces to cut down on wind and drafts during other seasons. Ultrashort blinds called *nokigake* are sometimes used to hide ugly views that can be seen from inside the house. In general, south-facing *sudare* are long while those made to face east are shorter as the sun never hits the bottom of these windows.

Yoshihiro sees *sudare* as a kind of social barometer: "Today there's less consideration, less kindness, and fewer *sudare*. Most traditional crafts are dying. This is the path that we Japanese are choosing, so it would be strange to complain. But as for me, I think life is important—you only live once. Making something beautiful and useful, something you can touch and see, that experience can't be bought with money. Anyway, talk to my son, he's twenty-eight and a mathematician. He went to a good university and worked for four years there, on his way to becoming a professor. Last year he decided to join us. I don't think family duty was the entire reason." His son's explanation was simple: whenever he thought about his future as a professor of mathematics, being a *sudare* artisan just seemed more interesting.

Asked how many *sudare* they made last year and what percent of this material was bamboo, cattail, or reed, Yoshihiro shrugs his shoulders. He and his father don't really keep track. They just order materials as they need them. He obviously doesn't think much of my question. Then he laughs and says, "You know, my mathematical son has been bothering me with the same kind of questions." One wonders in what ways Kotaro's mathematics will factor into the future of the Tanaka's *sudare*.

Tile Roofs

In the world of the clay roof, not much has happened for the past several hundred years. Some factories are automated, and there are modern flourishes such as brilliant blue, red, and green colored tiles. But the basic product is close to what it was in the sixth century, when *kawara* was introduced to Japan from China through Korea.

Kawara roofs were first used on temples. Then during the seventh century, people of rank were permitted to use *kawara* on their homes to symbolize their status, as later were the samurai of the Edo Period. In 1720, commoners were first allowed to use *kawara* as a fire prevention measure and after the big fire of 1792, *kawara* became obligatory on all new housing.

The original Japanese *kawara* roofing, called *honkawara-buki*, consisted of two pieces, one flatter than the other (see illustration). In 1674, lighter S-curve tiles called *sangawara* were invented, and at the end of the Edo Period projections were added to the bottom of these tiles so they could be hung on beams. This dispensed with the need for the heavy soil surface on which the tiles had been placed. Called *hikkake-sangawara*, or hanging tiles, they are the style used today. There are two kinds of *hikkake-sangawara*: *ibushi*, the traditional gray smoked-type, and *yuyaku*, the newfangled glazed ones.

Fujioka, a small town in Gunma Prefecture about three hours from Tokyo (by local train), has been in *kawara* production for twelve centuries. Since it's closer than the other major centers of Aichi, Hyogo, and Shimane prefectures, Itsuo and I set out to investigate roof tiles there. As we approached Fujioka on the

Hachiko Line, mountains loomed in the distance and rice, fruit, and vegetable fields dotted the landscape. Healthier and much more casual-looking school kids than you see in Tokyo slouched on the train seats, most without book bags, talking. More and more gray *kawara* roofs with their graceful aura of volume and strength came into view.

Fujioka's main streets have been cluttered by the usual urbanization, but the side streets with old homes sustaining magnificent gray carapaces flanked with ornaments and demons are of interest. Fujioka's sixty-three *kawara* makers in 1956 had shrunk to a mere seventeen by the beginning of 1994. There are still fewer today. Our first stop was at Fujioka Yogyo, a large two-story factory filled with machines that mix clay, and extrude and press tiles. These are then dried, coated, and transported downstairs to kilns where 8,000 tiles can be fired and dried at a time, a process that takes two days. Eight people work at the factory. Masao Kojima's business is streamlined, but production has decreased to 200,000 tiles from 500,000 tiles per month since 1975. Reasons for the decline, he says, include the proliferation of prefab homes, the development of new roofing materials, and obsessive rebuilding that obviates the need for roofs that last from forty to fifty years. He says that companies like Kubota and National are making new-style roofs (many with asbestos), and their large-scale promotion of their materials and links with construction companies are forcing *kawara* out of use. *Kawara*, he adds, tends to be cheaper than the new materials because the large companies corner the market and then set their prices.

The Igarashis run a more traditional business and make their tiles in the old manner, drying them outside over a period of days. The kiln they use is an old handmade one of clay, a *daruma-gama*. The smoke of pine wood gives their tiles a subdued gray look. They are one of only a handful of places where tiles are still made the original way. Three of them make about 120,000 *kawara* a year, a number which hasn't decreased over time. Because there are few places still faithful to old techniques, they are inundated with orders.

The Igarashis make all but the *onigawara*, or demon tiles, which are created by a specialist nearby. Lively, talkative—the antithesis of his grimacing demons—Shigeru Yamaguchi, a fifth-generation artisan, is the demon maker. These tiles protect a home from evil by scaring away bad luck and evil spirits. To protect the demon himself, a tubular projection, looking like a samurai's topknot, hovers over him to discourage bird droppings. A large demon can cost up to five million yen, but smaller ones, made with molds, can be had for as little as one thousand.

According to a survey released by the Ministry of International Trade and Industry (MITI), overall production of *kawara* has decreased since 1985. Of the *kawara* produced, *yuyaku*—the glazed type—had captured 68.3 percent of the total market by 1992, a large rise from a mere 26 percent in 1955. *Ibushi*, the traditional gray tiles, are down to 31.7 percent of the market. Tastes are changing. But some things haven't changed: the magnificent old roofing still lasts longer than needed, is environment friendly (can be recycled into roads), and contrary to popular belief costs less than its alternative.

HONKAWARA

SANGAWARA

HIKKAKE-SANGAWARA

Thatched Roofs

One thing you don't see very often these days is the *kayabuki yane*, or thatched roof, settled on top of a building like a well-barbered but bushy head of hair. The nation's architectural pate has, for the most part, balded and recent construction is paring down the few remaining pointed (albeit hairless) heads into flattops.

Across the road from the north exit of Chiba's Keisei Tsudanuma Station, a splendid example of the old *kayabuki* roof can be seen on top of a huge Edo Period residence. What's even more special, the place has remained a combination home and rice shop, despite its conven-ient location, spacious grounds, and the virulent *mansion* (condominium) virus all around. The Uekusa family crest, em-bedded in the roof above the front door, attests to a time when billboards were not plastic or neon, but made of natural materials, in this case bamboo.

As we sat at the *kotatsu* (a low, heated table) in the fifteen-mat room behind the rice shop chatting with the elder Mrs. Uekusa, her daughter-in-law served us tea. We were talking about thatched roofs. "You know," the younger woman broke in, "before I came here to marry, I was told that they were about to rebuild. My family, also, had just rebuilt their house, and I was quite happy at the prospect of living in a new place." She smiled with a touch of fatigue as she passed us sweets. "That was twenty-five years ago. All they rebuilt was the thatched roof. And what a production *that* was. It took six workers ten days or more. We not only put them up and paid them, but we had to provide them with an assortment of things like *zori* (Japanese-style sandals) and *tabi* (split-toed socks) for thanks as well."

Among the advantages of the thatched roof is the coolness it

provides during the summer humidity. Even in summers when the battle against mold is a nightmare due to unusual wetness, the Uekusas have no problem. The thatched roof is made-to-order for the Japanese climate, the perfect solution to many problems that plague us in more modern buildings. It insulates in the winter and keeps things cool in the summer. Of course, it is very flammable. And weeds and plants take root on the roof and have to be tended to.

What I wanted to know about was insects. Did they have bugs colonizing their ceiling? With a triumphant expression, the elder woman pronounced that she had actually found a few bugs that must have dropped off the ceiling the other day. Not nasty ones, but bugs just the same. In her long years of experience with thatched roofs, she says, this was the first time. Perhaps after twenty-five years, the roof needed tending. If only there was someone around who could do it.

"If cost were no object and you had to rebuild this house, what kind of place would you like?" I asked. The elder Mrs. Uekusa immediately pronounced, "No one is skilled enough to do it these days, but I'd like another house and roof just like this. After all, Japanese style is best for Japan." She looked up and around for a moment. "It's quite nice, isn't it, just as it is."

The younger woman was equally quick to answer. "I want a new house, a new and bright life. But I want a wooden home so we don't have to worry about our health. I worry about the new materials. I want two stories with lots of light, closets, and storage space. And a blue slate roof." She paused to catch her breath. "It's easier."

When her daughter-in-law left the room the elder Mrs. Uekusa lowered her voice conspiratorially. "I also came from a prosperous family that had the more modern roofs. When I came here as a bride, I was shocked to see this old thatched roof." She chuckled good-naturedly, "Oh, that was fifty-nine years ago."

Wooden Apartments

A few Meiji Era (1868–1912) *nagaya* (row houses) and some from the Taisho Era (1912–26) and Showa Era (1926–89) remain in Tokyo today. If you walk through the Taito Ward or Bunkyo Ward sections of *shitamachi* (old working-class neighborhoods) you can see some classic examples of all three styles. But you'd better take your walk soon, because these *nagaya* are fast being replaced by the tall, white, plastic-sided apartment buildings that are cropping up all over Tokyo.

Instituted in the Edo Period (1603–1868) as cheap housing for artisans, merchants, and day laborers, a *nagaya* is a long wooden building divided into sections that house individual families. Originally, each section had an entrance which served as a kitchen as well as a place to take off one's shoes, and a four-and-a-half-mat room beyond, where families of five and more lived. The narrow alleys within the compounds had a communal well, toilet, dumping ground, and a small shrine.

In the Taisho Era, the *nagaya* were bigger and had two stories. Back doors came into use and each unit had its own toilet. The first-floor front rooms of *nagaya* facing the streets were often used as workshops or small stores, as they still are today.

The earthquake of 1923 destroyed a large part of Tokyo, and the *nagaya* built after this were much larger than their predecessors—usually a six- and a two-mat room and independent kitchen on the ground floor, and a six-mat and a three-mat room above. The two- or three-mat kitchens were moved to the back and a small garden was grown in front beside the entrance. This garden was usually surrounded by a fence and somewhat obstructed the former easy communication between the separate sections.

The *nagaya* had a definite social role that has continued through to the present day. Groups of families living in the same building became a single family in terms of relationships and cooperation. Today, the situation hasn't changed much. The Spartan buildings are not luxurious or even comfortable. The summer heat forces everyone outside to talk and cool off in the evenings; the chill of winter prompts *nagaya* residents to linger and socialize in the warmth of the public bath before going to sleep. The walls are thin enough that neighbors are directly involved in each other's problems and activities. Perhaps because of this, *nagaya* life has been a central theme of modern *rakugo*, or comedy.

Relationships made in the *nagaya* are long-lasting and close. The *nagaya* lifestyle is a perfect antidote to the stress and pressure of fast-paced modern life. In the middle of Tokyo one can return from a hard day at work to a country-town atmosphere and a lot of neighbors who are more or less part of one's extended family. *Ninjo* is one of the words used to express this warmth and the interrelationships that are a characteristic feature of *shitamachi* neighborhoods and especially *nagaya* life.

The demolition of *nagaya* as well as other old housing is breaking up the communication in Tokyo's neighborhoods. With them are going the local street festivals, the public baths, and the warm sense of community that once was prevalent throughout Japan. Many people, including myself, pray that this distinctive way of life will survive the present construction boom.

3

Artisans and Crafts

Clogs

In Tokyo's *shitamachi* you will still see a line of geta at the entrances of the public baths in the evening. And occasionally an old man will clack down the street with panache, enjoying the resounding noise of his own passage.

The best geta are made of paulownia, a wood esteemed for its lightness, porosity, and beauty. The base and supports may be carved out of a single piece of wood or fashioned out of several pieces that are joined and glued. The strap of the geta, the *hanao*, is made of hemp, bamboo skin, or straw and is covered with cloth, silk, or leather.

The origin of geta is not certain. They probably first came to Japan from China, but they may have originated in Southeast Asia, India, or Africa, since all those places used geta-like shoes many centuries ago. But no matter where they came from, geta were more fully refined in their design and use in Japan than anywhere else in the world.

The development of geta seems to have centered around work in water. Clogs were used as far back as the Yayoi Period (300 B.C.–A.D. 300) by rice paddy workers. In feudal times they were used by people as they carried water, did the laundry, and were in the toilets. These geta were characterized by the height of their supports—a design developed to keep the feet clean and dry.

Children's geta have been found that date back to the Nara Period (710–94). Geta can also be seen in pictures of the Heian and Kamakura (1185–1336) periods, but it wasn't until the Edo Period (1603–1868) that geta became popular with just about everybody, rich and poor, and were used in nearly every activity, formal and informal. In fact, red-lacquered geta became so lavish

that the government prohibited their use for a short time in 1750.

Geta designs vary widely according to use. Some intriguing ones: 1) *pokkuri* are for young girls and *maiko* and have curved-in bottoms that create a beautiful noise when used; 2) *koshi* geta or *ashida* are for use in the rain; 3) *yuki* geta are designed so they don't catch or hold snow; 4) *mitsuba* geta were used for the *Oiran Dochu* ceremonial procession by first-class prostitutes; 5) *niwa* geta are for use in the garden; 6) *nori* geta are used in water by seaweed harvesters; 7) *suberi* geta are for skating; and 8) *butai* geta are used by Bunraku puppeteers.

Haruhiko Mizutani, owner of the Hasegawa Geta Shop in Taito Ward, says that geta shops remained very prosperous until about 1945, but by the late 1950s business had declined considerably. About this same time *zori* (formal kimono footwear), which had been less popular than geta, came into vogue. The decline in the use of geta was partly brought about by Westernization and partly by economics. *Zori* can be worn longer and, because of this, are more economical. Whereas Mr. Mizutani still has a clientele of specialists such as actors, actresses, priests, sumo wrestlers, and nightclub owners, today about 90 percent of his customers are housewives who buy *zori* .

One of the most famous clog shops in Tokyo, the Hasegawa Getaya has been in business since the beginning of the Meiji Era (1868–1912) when the shop was opened at Torigoe near Asakusa. A *norenwake* (branch store) was started at Daikongashi and it was through another *norenwake* that the present Hasegawa Shop was opened near Ueno Park sixty-three years ago. The shop is one of a very few that sells clogs that are handmade in the traditional way. Paulownia from Kitakata and Aizu (Fukushima Prefecture), which are said to have the best-quality trees in Japan, is used. Each of the three or four stages of cutting them into clogs is performed by a separate artisan, or *jikataya*. As there are no *jikataya* in Tokyo, the cutting is now done in Aizu. The *hanao* (straps), made by specialists called *hanaoya*, are slipped through three holes in the clogs with special tools and tied by Mr. Mizutani himself.

There is a man who sells cheap sandals out of a hand-pulled wooden cart near Ueno Park. If you ask him, he will let you paw through his wares. On the bottom of the heap, under mounds of vinyl and plastic-soled slippers, sometimes you can find a pair of beautifully grained paulownia clogs. "They don't sell anymore," he explained as he pulled out some ancient tools to strap in the *hanao* for me.

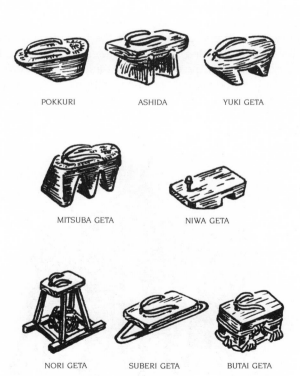

POKKURI   ASHIDA   YUKI GETA

MITSUBA GETA   NIWA GETA

NORI GETA   SUBERI GETA   BUTAI GETA

The Fire Brigade

A crowd of proud, tattooed men clash with a similar gang of toughs, issuing a barrage of insults. Street fighting by local fire brigades is a scene often found on the Kabuki stage. Even so, the fire-brigade tradition lives on, not just on the stages of traditional theater, but also through the Edo Shobo Kinenkai (Edo Fire Fighters Memorial Association).

The flavor of the former days is retained in the *dezomeshiki*, a yearly ritual in which members of the fire brigade show off their skills, balance, and daring. The fire brigades were organized in the Edo Period to combat the deadly conflagrations that periodically devastated Edo (today's Tokyo). The traditional wooden house of Japan is ideal in its resistance to wind, flood, and earthquake. But in the past, "great fires"—especially in the early months of the

year when the weather is dry and strong winds blow—burned so freely that houses weren't expected to last more than twenty years. In fact, fires were so frequent that they, along with the conflagrations between local fire teams, were dubbed the "Flowers of Edo."

Because no water or hoses were available, the main technique of fire fighting in those days was to contain the fire by chopping down the wooden houses surrounding the blaze. The special irony of this was that the fire fighters who tore down the buildings were also *tobishoku*, or builders. They were in effect tearing down what they would later be hired to rebuild. One wonders whether a conflict of interest might have been behind their reputation of being so quick and efficient.

Armed with nothing but *tobiguchi*, pickaxes made of wood and metal, they climbed up roofs on bamboo ladders and hacked away. They wore special clothing—pants and long *hanten* (jackets) made of quilted hemp (often with hand-painted *ukiyoe*-type scenes on the linings) that were wet down before use. The *zukin*, a hood that covered all but the eyes, was also fashioned out of the same hand-stitched material.

The Meiji Era brought many changes, including the Westernization of the fire-fighting system. Fire trucks, hoses, and water came into use. The *hikeshi* (traditional waterless fire fighter) days were over, but the Edo Shobo Kinenkai was formed to preserve the tradition. Every year in early January, there is a *dezomeshiki*, a flashy and dramatic acrobatic display of aerial daring at various locations in Tokyo. It is performed on seven-meter ladders made of bamboo and rope. While fifteen or so men secure the ladder with their *tobiguchi*, a man climbs up and balances himself on one of the poles in a flamboyant and daring pose. The pose is held for about half a minute, after which the man "falls" onto the top rung (with horrified gasps from the audience) and raises himself up into another, even more dramatic pose. And repeats the fall. There are no wires or nets to protect these men and the lopsided cantilevering poses are hard to believe. It's rather frightening to watch.

Katsumi Nakano is vice head of one of the four groups in Taito Ward. Years ago, when he was twenty, he fell while practicing a stunt. He hurt his foot so badly that he was out of work for almost two months. But he was lucky, he says. One of his colleagues died from a fall in 1951. It's dangerous: falls are not uncommon, and special insurance is taken out before performances. Of course, if the "firemen" aren't coordinated enough to do the stunts, they are relegated to singing or holding the ladder secure. But, as the group is made up of *tobishoku*, the construction men who work on the frames of tall buildings, to lack the requisite skill or daring to do acrobatics on the top of a ladder is a matter of humiliation.

The groups are organized in the same way as they were during the Edo Period. The stunts are done by *noriko*, and are preceded by two *matoimochi*, or standard-bearers, who display the symbol for their group. These *matoi* are whipped and twirled around as they walk through the streets before a demonstration. These same *tobishoku*, banded together as *hikeshi*, called out "*hi no yojin*" (beware of fires) in the evenings and acted as vigilantes from midnight to 5:00 A.M. in Asakusa up until the early 1970s. After midnight they would clack *hyoshigi* (wooden clappers) together to mark the time without calling out.

These and other community services were the domain of the *tobishoku* and done free of charge. The Edo Shobo Kinenkai members are as proud of their daring and their image today as were the fire fighters of old Edo, and it's their highly regarded place in the community that gives them their pride. These last independent *tobishoku* who still act as *hikeshi* are vestiges of a warmer, more connected, and certainly more daring lifestyle.

Will Mr. Nakano's son continue on in his father's footsteps? Mr. Nakano shakes his head sadly, "He's gone to a university—he's studying. I started this work at sixteen Technique was everything then, not certificates as it is today. Kids get taught in school to want diplomas. But who knows? Maybe he will join us once he's finished his studies."

MATOI

Perfection of Skill

In the front room of an old wooden house, its ceiling sagging with age, Sukeshiro Tagami stands in rapt concentration at his wood lathe. As the bowl he is working on turns on the wheel, he holds a metal tool steadily against the wood causing chips and slivers to fly. The door of his shop is always partly open and the yellow glare of the light bulb directly above him competes with the shadows at the back of the room that are ever so slightly flickering against row upon row of handmade tools. Long after sunset, Mr. Tagami remains at his job, immune to both heat and bitter cold, always working, always busy.

It isn't in his nature to sit around and relax, and when he sat down to talk with me on Sunday, his day off, he was constantly jumping out of his chair to look for this and that to show me. Among his treasures are commemorative postcards that had been issued at the deaths of the Meiji and Taisho emperors and other documentary cards showing dead bodies heaped in piles after the Great Kanto Earthquake of 1923. He lived through these events and collected the cards himself. From a large box he pulled out a beautiful collection of *natsume*, the decorative containers used in the tea ceremony to hold powdered tea, some thin

glass holders, MacArthur-style pipes, and elegant bowls and trays. All were objects that he had made himself.

An energetic ninety-three, Sukeshiro Tagami is one of a handful of living artisans trained in the traditional and backbreaking style. The few younger craftsmen, his son included, who are carrying on old crafts have undergone arduous training to be sure, but nothing that compares with the long, severe apprenticeships of the past.

The fourth son of a farming family, Mr. Tagami had to find a profession. As was the custom, his oldest brother alone would inherit the entire farm. Thus, at the age of fifteen, he went to Tokyo to apprentice himself to an established wood craftsman. For seven years he worked, receiving an occasional allowance, nothing more. At twenty-two, when he had finished his apprenticeship, he spent a year working for his master without pay in thanks for his training, and then began regular employment. It wasn't until he was twenty-eight years old that he felt qualified to open his own shop. According to him, it takes eight years or more to become a real artisan.

For eight years, Mr. Tagami was up and peddling a mechanical lathe before dawn. A normal workday would start before daybreak and end at 10:00 or 11:00 P.M. At the end of the year, however, it was not uncommon for him to work around the clock to complete orders. He got the first and the fifteenth of every month off, but he had to repair his own tools and do personal errands during this time. He was never allowed out at night. I asked him what he did for pleasure in those days. After thinking for a while he replied, "Eat. Eating was our only pleasure. We were provided with a tiny allowance and maybe once a month we went out for a bowl of *udon* (noodles) or *gyudon* (a bowl of rice and meat)." How about drinking and smoking, I inquired. He chortled, "I still don't smoke—no time to. And drinking, well, in those days I hadn't so much as even *seen* saké."

It's hard to think of Mr. Tagami's work as "products" because they are made with so much care and skill. He is able to carve wood so thin that you can see through it as if it were lace. Perhaps there is no one else in the world who can use a lathe in such a way.

Last night, around ten, I passed his home on my way back from the public bath. I heard the whir of his lathe. The door was open as usual, and the yellow light glared out at me. Mr. Tagami's shadow stretched out the door, across my path. In the perfection of a craft, this same shadow has been stretching thus for the past seventy-eight years.

NATSUME

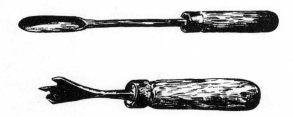

Japanese Umbrellas

Some eyebrows were raised when the present Emperor and Empress held their own umbrellas at Emperor Hirohito's funeral. In Japan, umbrellas have many uses—symbolic and otherwise—but the thing that surprises me most about them is that their original use was to shield one from the sun, not the rain. "Umbra," after all, means shade in Latin.

There are all sorts of umbrellas: they come plain and rococo, large and small, and are made with a variety of materials including plastic, polyester, and nylon. Truly one-of-a-kind is the Japanese-style umbrella (*wagasa*) which is made of oiled rice paper and has lacquered spokes and a plain wood or bamboo handle. An authentic, handmade *wagasa* is hard to find, and once found, sometimes even more difficult to buy.

Takeshi Yabuta is making the real McCoy right here in Tokyo, no plastic handles, metal parts, or modern doodads at all. But unless your name is Tamasaburo or Kikugoro, you don't have much of a chance of getting one of these. And it's not the price that I'm talking about. Despite thirty-some years of experience and being recognized as an intangible cultural asset, Mr. Yabuta sells his masterpieces for a modest 13,000 to 15,000 yen. A true artisan, he is as proud of his low prices as he is of his skill.

Sitting cross-legged with a purple cloth spread over his knees, Mr. Yabuta flicked the ashes of his cigarette into the small hibachi at his side. The butts were meticulously placed in another ashtray. "I learned my craft at the theater. My family has specialized in Kabuki umbrellas for four generations." His arms rested sensually on his thighs. He spoke with the charisma of a successful Kabuki actor.

"Three different artisans used to be involved in making the umbrellas—the spoke carver, the paper paster, and the one who finished things up. But when you work that way you end up not being able to do anything on your own. I get my paper, high-quality *kozo*, from Gosuke Kikuchi. He's an intangible cultural asset as well and makes the best *washi* available. But I carve and lacquer the bones (spokes) myself, paste the paper, and cut the handles."

He handed me a huge purple umbrella with the Ichikawa seal on it, and smiled smugly at my surprise. It was feather-light. "Danjuro used this in *Sukeroku*," he said. The feel of his umbrellas is like velvet. They settle into your hand, they are light and airy, smooth and special. Gifu is famous for its *wagasa* and I have held many umbrellas made there but the feeling of Mr. Yabuta's is entirely different: noticeably lighter, smoother—a pampered, refined feeling. The lack of plastic and modern parts is not half of the difference. I instantly understood why this man is making all of the umbrellas used in Kabuki today.

"Kabuki actors are no longer so close to artisans," he said slipping off again to a Kabuki tangent. "Uzaemon is my friend but, in general, contact has dried up." Reaching into a drawer he pulled out two small silver and gold *kiseru* (thin, long pipes). "Kikugoro VI gave these to me. He was a friend. And I have kept the *sandangasa*, the three-tiered umbrella that my grandfather invented and Kikugoro used. These are my real treasures."

Before he starts an umbrella he needs to know the name of the play, the role, and the specific actor who is going to perform it. "The really difficult part," he says, "is balance. If it is a large man playing a female part, I make a large umbrella to make him appear smaller. And vice versa. The size of props is very important. And you've noticed the symbolism, haven't you? Umbrellas held over a person are used to designate his rank. A *bangasa* (the large, thick *wagasa* as opposed to the *janome* which is thinner and more feminine) that is ripped tells us that this is a man who is about to fall from his elevated, noble station . . . . There are so many symbolic uses of *wagasa* in Kabuki."

The room was full of little brushes, blades, special tweezers, hammers with cork heads, piles of bamboo, even a hair dryer. Umbrellas were hanging in purple bags like bats from the ceiling. "What kind of umbrella do you usually use yourself?" I asked him. "One of those regular black Western types," he said and continued on about Kabuki.

Cotton Kimono

Twelve-meter strips of patterned cloth billow in the wind like the colorful spinnakers of sailboats—red, navy, emerald green, and pink. It's a delightful sight, the cloth snapping in the breeze on a hot summer morning. But these are not the sunny shores of California; we're a muggy three-minute walk from Kita Senju Station at the Okamura Dyeing Factory in downtown Tokyo. Beneath the flying colors are a huge, wooden factory, a large open space, and a modern office building flanked by still another old building for storage. Off to the side at the entrance are a series of steel drums fitted with complicated valves. A concession to modern times, they were put in a little over ten years ago to remove chemicals from the waste water. This factory has been adding color to natural fibers for more than half a century. They specialize in *tenugui*, the long thin cloth that is worn around the head during local festivals and that is still given as a gift at traditional dance and music recitals. *Yukata* fabric is another specialty, and business is booming. Anybody who has been to a large event in the summer will have noticed: young ladies are taking to the streets in fancy *yukata* ensembles—some costing 30,000 yen and more.

Yukata date back to the Heian Period (794–1185) when they were called *yukatabira* and were worn by the modest upper classes while bathing. By the Edo Period, the *yukata* had filtered down to less modest commoners who wore them after their baths, as a kind of bathrobe. These days, they are provided to customers at hotels and inns for use as pajamas. But other than this use as pajamas, the *yukata* has become the ultimate fashion to wear out on a summer date.

For Itsuo Okamura, president and owner of the dyeing factory, this is wonderful news. His factory was in full swing with twenty-nine workers dyeing and rinsing out fabrics. As *yukata* are informal, unlined, cotton kimono that are worn mainly in the summer, material made for them must be ordered and prepared before

May. March and April are their busiest months. Orders for "eld-erly" patterns are down while those for young women are surging. Several years ago, geometric patterns were in, but now the major-ity of orders are for traditional flower patterns—morning glories and hydrangea—and butterfly patterns, old standards, but in non-traditional colors. Mr. Okamura says his company uses about 600 different patterns a year, 70 to 80 percent of which are new. Their beautiful wooden factory is piled high with pristine white rolls of 100 percent cotton cloth; they use no synthetic materials.

Traditionally, *yukata* fabrics were dyed in indigo, but these days a host of other colors, up to ten per fabric, are also added. Even so, the basic process hasn't changed a great deal. The Okamura Factory uses the *chusen* method where twelve-meter bolts of cotton cloth are folded fan-style in meter-long lengths. The folded fabric is placed on a waist-high machine. Using stencils prepared by specialists, the worker spreads a brownish paste onto the folded fabric over the stencil with a long wooden tool. The paste resists the dye to form the patterns. Then dye is sprayed onto the folded cloth while a pedal-operated suction device pulls it through the twelve layers. For a simple indigo pattern, this is the end of the process and the cloth is then dropped into a stream for rinsing. (The stream is now a horseshoe-shaped, man-made one fitted with special handles that shake the cloth in the water. And the colored waste water is carefully filtered before it is returned to the community water system.) The final process is hanging the long strips out above the factory to dry in the sun. About 500 twelve-meter bolts can be produced in one day.

The fabric patterns used in hotel and inn *yukata* are often machine-made. By looking closely at the folds of the material, one can judge whether they are hand-dyed or not. It takes one 12-meter-by-40-centimeter cloth strip, called a *tan*, to make a single *yukata*. As mentioned earlier, meter lengths are folded under each other during dyeing. At these folds in hand-dyed fabrics—in exactly one-meter segments—the pattern is interrupted ever so slightly and reversed from the folded edge. Machine-made patterns have no such interruption and are uniformly perfect throughout.

What is behind the current boom in *yukata*? It is difficult to say. Production peaked during the 1964 Olympics when 13,027,972 *tan* were produced. In 1987 production was at an all-time low of 242,217 *tan*. Since then, however, sales have been increasing by leaps and bounds. Suddenly, *yukata* have became fashionable wear for the young (as opposed to traditional wear for the elderly)—especially for viewing summer fireworks and attending parties. Production has jumped but not nearly enough to meet demand. The big dilemma that dyers now face is whether or not to make large investments for increasing production to meet this new demand. Will this boom last, or is it the swan song of the *yukata* trade?

Edo-Style Joiners

In times past, the birth of a daughter was heralded by planting a paulownia seedling in the garden. By the time she turned sixteen and was ready for marriage, the paulownia had matured and was ready to be fashioned into a chest of drawers to accompany her to her new home. The preparation of the chest was the work of a joiner. Drawers would be fitted together so exactly that they would slide open and shut effortlessly. They were assembled without the aid of nails or glue.

Saw-toothed connections of all shapes and descriptions are the bones and cartilage of joinery work; they are what give a chest of drawers, box, or makeup stand its strength and durability. And they are the secret to judging the quality of fine furniture. A joiner is always searching for a better connection, a better way to put things together.

Joinery work in Japan goes back well over a thousand years. The eighth-century double-doored containers for Buddhist images were the products of joiners. Later, in the twelfth century special artisans called *hakotsukuribe* formed a guild that made platforms for futon, portable Chinese chests, folding tables, and other furnishings used by the Imperial Court, the nobility, and the feudal lords. The Momoyama Period in the latter half of the sixteenth century brought a long interval of peace, and with it, a renaissance that included elaborate furniture and things made of wood.

Edo sashimono, or Edo woodworking, is the quintessence of elegance and restraint. Because it developed in association with the Spartan samurai ethic, it is a strong contrast to the elaborate woodwork that developed in the Kansai region. Among the shogunate and its following that moved to Edo grew a simple and elegant style that came to be known as "Edo taste," a style notable for its lack of decoration and showy elements. It was reverse snob appeal of a sort; the valuable, most beautiful parts of things were kept hidden. Only those with special knowledge could appreciate their worth. Thus silk kimono were woven to look like ordinary cloth; a plain-looking outer coat would have an exquisite pattern on the inside where only the owner could see. And in furniture, it was only by inspecting the joints or attachments and the natural grain of the wood that one could ascertain its intrinsic worth. Joiners competed with each other by inventing ingenious joints

that could not be seen from the outside. It was austere, elegant dignity—so different from the taste of Kansai that was influenced by the indulgent, sometimes flamboyant tastes of the Imperial Court. This was the origin of *iki*, an almost untranslatable word whose meaning encompasses elegance, simplicity, and refinement.

There are only twenty masters of E*do sashimono* alive today. The youngest is Toshio Toda, born in 1951, who lives in a two-story wooden home in Negishi. He became an E*do sashimono* joiner quite by chance. His high school teacher arranged for him to apprentice himself to Kuniharu Shimazaki, the most famous Edo-style joiner then alive. He was trained in the traditional way, living with Shimazaki for seven years, from the age of eighteen. He started out by just cleaning the work area and his teacher's house. Time passed and he was allowed to polish the objects his teacher had made. Still more time passed before he was allowed to make his own tools and actually start. His first creation was a pair of chopsticks.

As in Edo times, he learned indirectly by "stealing" techniques from his teacher. He was not told or shown how to do anything. Rather, he watched what was going on around him and gradually mastered techniques through observation. "My *oyakata* (teacher) was more strict about manners, about my lining up the shoes of guests correctly, treating my *senpai* (elders) properly, and greeting

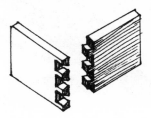 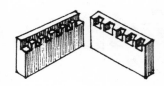

fellow workers and customers politely than about work techniques. But we knew if we weren't strict with ourselves we would never succeed. That was our strongest motivation."

Mr. Toda sat cross-legged on the wooden workshop floor in front of a dresser that he was crafting. His walls are littered with handmade tools and corners are piled with large pieces of wood drying. Outside the house, too, there are stacks of wood, carefully protected from sun and rain, drying. To prevent his furniture from warping, he will dry his wood from two to thirty years. Favored wood has beautiful grain: mulberry, pear, Japanese cedar, paulownia, or zelkova. Somewhat like an experienced wine taster, Mr. Toda can sense the quality and state of his wood through the physical aspects of its color and feel.

After our talk, Mr. Toda took me upstairs where he had some of his work on display. The small room literally sparkled with handsome polished wood: dressers, low tables, cupboards with secret spring drawers, and hibachi. Each piece had a dignity of its own. Any one of the objects by itself would furnish a room. You don't even have to see the joinery to appreciate them—strength and elegance just emanate from these simple objects. They even have an element of mystery: how does he get those beveled mirrors into their one-piece wooden frames without the use of glue or joints?

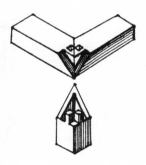

Portable-Shrine Makers

Standing in a pile of lacy shavings and grinning, Tokuji Ai admits that it was purely by chance that he became a *miyashi*. "My father was a farmer and I was his second son, so I had to take up some sort of craft." His work, which he proceeded to show us in album after album of pictures, as if he were introducing his family, consists of handsome lacquered *mikoshi*, outdoor shrines, wooden decorations and shrines for wedding halls, and the *kamidana* that preside in a high corner of almost every house in Japan.

The *mikoshi*, or "palanquin of the gods," is a highly ornate miniature replica of a shrine, usually with a gilded phoenix on its roof, that rests on two long horizontal poles. Prior to its development, a mirror and a branch of the *sakaki* tree had been paraded around on horseback as a symbol of divine presence. The first recorded use of today's palanquin-like structure was in the transfer of a Kyushu shrine deity and sacred texts to Nara where they were to safeguard the construction of the Great Buddha image at the Todaiji temple in 749. By the tenth century it had become common practice in Kyoto to placate the malevolent spirits believed to cause epidemics by carrying deities through its communities in *mikoshi*. In the twelfth and thirteenth centuries, *mikoshi* from the powerful Buddhist temples Enryakuji and Kofukuji were jounced through Kyoto to intimidate government authorities into accepting the demands of the temples.

Even today, the *mikoshi* is raucously carried through city wards on the shoulders of twenty or thirty people dressed in special

festival clothing. The carriers shout *"soiya, soiya!"* as they move in unison. The *mikoshi* is carried in a zigzag fashion with a bouncy flourish called the *mikoshi furi* which is said to show the turbulent character of the deity enshrined within. This deity will then extend its protection to the neighborhood. The more energetically the *mikoshi* is tossed and shaken, the more realistically the gilded phoenix on top flaps its wings and "flies." During festivals, the heavy *mikoshi* are intermittently placed in temporary resting places, *otabisho*, where locals provide saké and food, and neighborhood elders, clad in their local-patterned yukata, preside.

There are countless special tools, chisels, saws, and planes hanging on the walls of the Bunkyo Ward workshop—and a few electric saws as well. Mr. Ai hands me a shaving to inspect. It's of Japanese cypress, the main and only material along with the tougher zelkova tree that is used to make the body of the shrines. It's so thin that it's transparent and as soft and delicate as old lace. The strong, sweet aroma of cypress permeates the rooms. "It takes about a year to make a large *mikoshi*," Mr. Ai continues. "Orders are usually made in the fall, after the large festivals. Mr. Hosoda and I can make about two or three a year. But it's not just us, the *kijiya* (wood workers), there are other artisans involved: the *chokinya* (decorative metal workers); the *urushiya* (lacquerers); and the *hakuya* (goldbeaters). But we take the order, carve the parts, send them off to the other artisans, and then assemble the pieces as the last step. We see it through the whole process."

"Our customers are mostly private individuals—and companies like Seibu. The shrines on top of the Seibu Department Stores are all ours. The work isn't really dying out—I don't think it ever will completely because it's part of Shinto, which permeates our lives. But it seems to have reached a peak about ten years ago with all the rebuilding of hotels and large buildings. They all have wedding halls, you know. Before the wedding hall business started thirty years ago, people were married at the shrine or at home.

"There aren't many *miyashi* in Tokyo anymore. Maybe five or six in Asakusa, and I have ten *deshi* (apprentices). Gradually, I suppose, regular carpenters will start doing the work. We use no nails; instead we make hundreds of little wooden clasp-like parts. And then we fit them all together. It's quite a job."

Mr. Ai's apprenticeship started when he was sixteen. His training involved working from 4:00 A.M. until at least 10:00 P.M., all but two days a month. For this he received a small allowance which he would spend on his two free days in Asakusa, at the theaters because it wasn't enough money to go out drinking. Many of his fellow apprentices quit. When he turned twenty, his formal training ended, after which he worked for his teacher for a year without pay, a custom called *oreiboko*. It wasn't until ten years after he had started that he considered himself a real *miyashi*.

"I'm seventy-seven years old, so I've been working at this sixty years now," he said. He looks like he might be in his fifties, and when I mentioned this he replied, "Oh, that's because I enjoy my work. To be truthful, I wouldn't want to be a businessman or anything else. They have to retire at fifty-five. Then what can they do? Work part time or just fool around. I'm lucky. I can continue doing what I love to do. One thing that is hard, though, is when my work is sold through someone else and I lose track of where it is." He rubs the edges of his photo albums as he says this. "When I don't know where they are . . . I really dislike that."

MIKOSHI

Woodblock Prints

Senrei Sekioka makes his living by reproducing prints of Sharaku and Utamaro and making the name stickers that get pasted on temple gates. He's a fifth-generation woodblock printer; his family's printing tradition traces back to 1781. Not only does he have apprentices, but he is also a lecturer at the Musashino University of Art, and Arakawa Ward has made video after video about him and his craft. He is enormously successful and busy, but rather than enjoying his success, he remains dissatisfied. "Just when Japan has become so rich, everybody's buying European art—like van Goghs for eighty-some million dollars. That kind of thing is really abnormal. Japanese people don't appreciate their own art. It's disappointing."

Mr. Sekioka's dream is to put the "art" back into woodblock printing. A veteran artisan of forty-five years, he makes a clear distinction between an artisan and an artist, and what each is capable of doing. The explanation goes back to the seventeenth century when woodblock prints first became popular, continues through the following century, and culminates in *ukiyoe* prints. These prints were the products of publishing houses. The now famous woodblock prints were not the work of single artists, but resulted from the cooperation of four people. The most important of the four was the publisher, who commissioned, paid for, and decided what was to be printed in the first place. Prints were made to be sold at a high volume and at a low price, similar to the signed star photographs that are sold at theaters today.

The artists, or "illustrators" as Mr. Sekioka calls them, had none of the importance that we now attach to them. Hiroshige, Utamaro, they were only one step in a process. They took the order and made a sketch that was handed to the carver, who then made a series of blocks, the number of which depended on the number of colors used in the print. The blocks were handed from the carver over to the printer, who made the prints in editions of two hundred. Once the two hundred were sold, two hundred more were printed up. According to Mr. Sekioka, they had to sell about two thousand to really make a profit in those days.

The high quality of the *ukiyoe* prints thus developed from the skill and cooperation of four people, not the talent of one artist. It was only in cases where the publisher had good business sense, and the artist, carver, and printer were highly skilled, that the prints hold value today. The carvers and printers spent their entire lives perfecting their crafts. Apprenticeship lasted seven years for the carver and six for the printer, after which many years of daily work ensued before they measured up to the exacting standards of those days. If any one of the four men involved was wanting in ability, then an excellent print could not be made.

"Today, young artists make the picture and try to do the carving and the printing themselves," Mr. Sekioka comments. "An expert can easily tell that the workmanship is inferior and, of course, this is to be expected. No matter how creative the picture or the idea, the result is never very good. Artists don't have the time to perfect either carving or printing; they can't hope to compete with an artisan who has spent his entire life doing nothing but carving or printing. It can't be helped."

"Artisans like me are not artists, either. We don't have the creativity to make a good base picture. Reproducing things of high quality is our job, and it isn't easy by any means. This is where the problem arises. Reprints of old *ukiyoe* are what we are doing. They sell. But they have no artistic value, no matter how technically brilliant our work is. Copies are copies. What I want to do is to print modern, original works. Use our old and very successful system to produce modern prints of the very highest quality, ones that an artist could never do by himself."

Mr. Sekioka has, in fact, made some modern woodblock prints. A series of modern Kabuki actors—Ennosuke, Danjuro, and Kikugoro, for example—the colors and designs of which are beautiful. But the faces, Mr. Sekioka himself admits, have no character when compared to a Sharaku or Utamaro. They are too "pretty." And the subject matter is dated. He has also produced and printed prints with the famous *nihonga* artist Hosei Jimbo, with Hambei Okura as the carver. But the artist is eighty-two years old and he does pictures of traditional kimonoed females. "If only he would do modern women," Mr. Sekioka says with a sigh. Another artist, Seiichiro Ono, has done a print of a street scene in Tokyo, but none of these sell really well, despairs Mr. Sekioka. "Japanese like designer goods. If it's a woodblock print then it has to be *ukiyoe*."

It is sad that what may be the last generation of properly trained carvers and printers may die out without having had the chance to produce first-rate original works. Today's up-and-coming artists should take this opportunity to make technically brilliant woodblock prints while there are still artisans who can produce them.

Name Stickers

Senja fuda are Japan's rendition of graffiti—a neater way of leaving one's name or mark, without spray paint and without making a mess. And just as the fabled graffiti artists Chaka and Ozone in Los Angeles, *senja fuda* aficionados aim for the most out-of-the-way, difficult places to affix their signatures, leaving us to puzzle over how they got there. But *senja fuda* has quite a few centuries' start on graffiti that was born in the South Bronx of New York City only a few decades ago.

If you have visited any temples or shrines in Japan then you have surely seen entrance gates plastered with small slips of paper bearing neat black kanji. There are two distinct types of *senja fuda*: *daimei nosatsu* and *kokan nosatsu*. The former are those name stickers on the gates; the latter are more elaborate prints that are exchanged between people.

The origin of *senja fuda* stretches back to Heian times when pilgrimages were made to worship Kannon, the Buddhist goddess of mercy. Names, addresses, and a prayer for a good life both now and after death were written on wooden slats that were hung by bamboo nails to the gates of Kannon temples. Pilgrimages were originally made by the nobility to a set thirty-three temples but, gradually, visiting Inari shrines became popular and the practice of *senjamode*, or visiting one thousand shrines for luck and the charity of the gods, came into being. The name *senja fuda*

comes from this custom. *Senja* means a thousand shrines and *fuda* means card. Pilgrims pasted them on the ceilings and pillars of shrines and temples as symbols of their piety. The custom started as a religious one, but by the Edo Period it had filtered down from the nobility to become a popular form of recreation for the common man.

Pasting *senja fuda* in out-of-the-way places became a fashion and prints gradually included puns and humor. Tea houses with beautiful women invariably sprang up next to the temples and shrines so what little that was left of the notion of pray turned quickly into play.

The *senja fuda* themselves changed from prayers on wood to handwritten names on rice paper to, finally, the woodblock print versions you see today. The majority were black and white, although there were some colored ones. As with clothing and other things, gradually the Edo government enacted laws about how elaborate these *senja fuda* could be. And, as with hairstyles and kimono patterns, one was allowed certain colors and patterns according to one's rank and station in life. In Edo times, one glance at a fabric pattern along the edges of tatami, at a female's hairdo, or at a kimono would peg the owner or household to a certain rung that was determined and maintained by law.

Well now, how do those names reach such high and out-of-the-way places? Proper pilgrims, even today, carry a prayer scroll, prayer beads, a bell, a fold-out book for 300-yen shrine and temple stamps, a wooden box packed with *senja fuda*, and a tin can full of paste. They dress in white with straw hats and footwear. Many weigh themselves down further with a walking staff. But the secret to out-of-the-way access is a collapsible rod—some are said to be eight meters in length. These rods have two brushes called *meotobake* positioned at about thirty degrees to each other with a clip on the other side of the brushes. Paste is first brushed on the back of the print which is then clasped against the top of the rod. The rod is pressed against the desired position and then rolled back so that the brushes smooth it against the wood of the gate.

Today's paste isn't particularly good for wood (they used to use rice mush) and temple priests are not pleased when visitors paste without praying or purchasing a stamp. Senrei Sekioka, Japan's leading expert on *senja fuda*, says that young people aren't going about things properly. Prayer wasn't particularly important in the Edo Period either but at least they went through the motions, he comments. Once pasted, the signs last a long time. He claims there are Edo Period prints on the Daijiji gate in Chichibu. The one he pasted there thirty years ago still remains as well. The paper gradually disappears but the *sumi* ink is absorbed into the wood as if it had been directly written on it.

If temple-hopping strikes you as a hobby worth pursuing, you can have your own *senja fuda* made in original woodblock form. I have been toying with the idea of ordering some with the kanji for "smokestack" to stick on the backs of clandestine subway smokers, but even this little bit of fun comes at a price. Real *senja fuda* are printed as they were several hundred years ago, in lots of two hundred. And they're the work of three professionals: a letterer, a wood carver, and a printer. Mr. Sekioka says it can be done in pure Edo form for 21,000 yen. But the paste, collapsible rod, wooden box, and snazzy white outfit are extra.

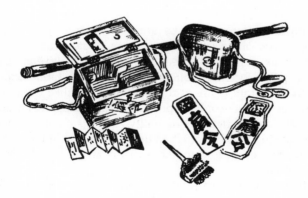

Edo Taste

Throughout Japanese history there has been a tendency in the common man toward elaboration and show, and outbursts of flamboyance were time and again outlawed by the government. Lavish tastes in kimono caused the Edo (old Tokyo) government to forbid the use of ornate patterns and expensive materials, and these ordinances helped to create the refined "Edo taste." A glimpse of the true heart of the people could be seen, however, in a peek at the lining of a kimono coat. The outward plain fabric of a merchant's wear was a legislated surface suppressing a flashy interior of fancy patterns and expensive materials in the linings. In the same way, gradually people began to have their *senja fuda* made more and more elaborately, until, instead of pasting them on gates, they began to exchange them with others. This new custom caught on quickly and people organized groups called *ren* which ordered elaborate prints made with beautiful, dynamic designs and colors instead of just calligraphy. Names were still printed, but ostentatious pictures soon became a popular focus.

This new type of *senja fuda* called *kokan nosatsu* was strongly influenced by *ukiyoe* prints. These increasingly large and elaborate woodblock prints became collector's items, and *kokan nosatsu* became an important genre of the *ukiyoe* print. Unlike the *ukiyoe* print, however, they were ordered privately by individuals or groups, thus affording a great deal of originality. Artisans had more freedom in producing these prints than in the case of standard *ukiyoe* which were checked by government censors and sold publicly in large numbers.

As with other woodblock prints the *kokan nosatsu* were made by a group of cooperating artisans, all of whom held equal importance in the process. There was a calligrapher, an illustrator, a carver, a printer, and sometimes even a professional storyteller (to help with the puns and witticisms) working together to make the pictures. Now-famous names like Hiroshige, Eisen, Kunisada,

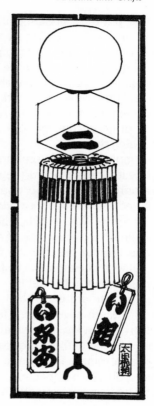

and Kuniyoshi produced beautiful *senja fuda* for private collectors. Most of the *ukiyoe* artists were working on *kokan nosatsu* by the end of the Edo Period and these prints were highly competitive with commercial *ukiyoe*. They ended up influencing not only *ukiyoe* prints but also pictures for toys, games, and books.

Collector-organized *ren* worked with artists and storytellers to create original pictures that had a sense of wittiness (*share*) and chic (*iki*). They held meetings periodically where they would deliver the prints to their members. In fact, the oldest surviving invitation card to one of these meetings dates back to 1799. First held at private homes and temples, the meetings then shifted to new venues such as expensive tea houses and restaurants until, once again, the government thought things were getting out of hand and prohibited them in this same year. But, as with so many government restrictions, this proved only temporary. As the collectors' prints became more and more elaborate, so did the act of exchanging them.

The import of Western culture and printing techniques after the Meiji Restoration marked the start of the decline of handmade *ukiyoe* prints. People who wanted to keep Edo traditions alive continued to exchange *senja fuda* through organized meetings. The first big revival was in 1880, followed by another in the Taisho Era (1912–26) when a new type of artist, the *nihonga* artist, started to make designs for the collector prints. Another revival is occurring now, but with questionable taste, according to Senrei Sekioka, the foremost expert in the field.

Today there are more than thirty groups in Tokyo (since the Meiji Era there have been a few in the Kansai region, but this tradition was and is still primarily an Edo custom). Mr. Sekioka is involved in one of these groups whose members meet four times a year at a temple in Ueno. Caretakers choose subjects for the pictures, but the number and size of the pictures depends on the group's budget. For example, in a group with 450 members, if each member pays 6,000 yen there is a budget of 2,700,000 yen. One set of prints may cost about 300,000 yen, so the 450 members could make nine different prints. Each series will carry one-ninth of the members' names, or fifty names. Each member will get a set of nine prints, but only one of these will bear the member's name. At these meetings, some members exchange their own personal *senja fuda* as well.

According to Mr. Sekioka there is a boom in these *kokan nosatsu* right now. What is lacking, he says, is the quality—the ability to express witticism and chic in the prints. Many of today's collectors are young: they don't understand past traditions and they haven't developed an aesthetic sense. As a result, the quality of the prints has gone down. The humor, intellect, fashion, and surprise of the *kokan nosatsu* are gone. In their place is just a pretty picture and a lot of names.

Paper Mounters

One big obstacle to the growth of Western art in Japan has been the size of Japanese homes; there isn't much space in them to hang pictures. This space limitation is behind the success of the decorative sliding doors, screens, and the traditional *kakejiku*, or hanging scroll. These are all media that either become part of the functional structure of a room or a compact, seasonal object that can be reduced in size and stored easily. Japanese calligraphy, scroll paintings, and screen paintings are all similar in that they require the attention of a *hyogushi* to mount them and keep them clean and in good shape.

Hyogushi are also called *kyojiya* today, although the names have different origins. Sutra were introduced with Buddhism in the mid–sixth century, and mounting them became important work. The artisans involved prospered and by the late Heian Period (twelfth century) they were called *kyojiya*. Independent of this, changes in lifestyle and houses and the creation of the tea ceremony encouraged the development of *kakejiku*, *byobu* (folding screens), *fusuma* (sliding doors), books, and so on, with pictures as well as calligraphy on them. This was the realm of the *hyogushi*. During the Edo Period the work of the *kyojiya* and *hyogushi* became mixed until there was no distinction between them at all. The present building frenzy has caused many *hyogushi* to tackle interior decoration—a new path—rather than scrolls, *byobu*, and *fusuma*. For this reason, the numbers of *hyogushi* show little attrition: about 700 in Tokyo alone and 7,000 throughout the country. But those attending to the original work of the *hyogushi* are few and far between.

Although the specialists that purge the bugs and scrape off the mold of centuries from precious museum pieces are few, they're in great demand. Hiroyoshi Ishii concentrates on calligraphy and Buddhist scrolls. Working with his eighty-three-year-old father in Tokyo's Ueno area, he represents the fifteenth generation of the

Ishii family occupied with this work. As generations before them, they mount artwork on scrolls—an exacting art in itself. But their business today is slanted heavily toward renovation: washing and repairing old and sometimes priceless works of art. Unlike in

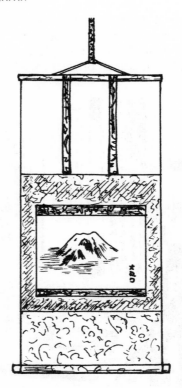

other countries, in Japan there is no formal "school" training for renovation skills such as de-molding, de-bugging, purging stains and water marks and wrinkles, or repairing rips and tears. The artworks come from museums and temples as well as from private homes to be treated with a combination of generations-old techniques (like using charcoal flakes to wash paper) and modern chemicals in the transformation back to their original form.

The Ishiis have unwrapped an extraordinary handwritten book that dates from the Genroku Era (1688–1704) to show us the condition of some of the materials they restore. Handwritten in flowing black ink, it is a record of *yomeiri dogu*, the possessions that a bride takes with her to her new family when she marries. Some of the pages are in shreds and the top page glistens with mold. They will wash it page by page and line each with new *washi*. The process will take about a year of painstaking labor; theirs is an occupation where even the slightest mistake can ruin a masterpiece. Scrolls are laid on two low wooden tables in the tatami-floored workshop while work is done on them. Hanging on boards from the ceiling and walls like negatives in a darkroom are countless pictures and calligraphy taped up to dry.

Part of the challenge these days is to obtain suitable materials: the brocaded fabrics from Kyoto for the *kakejiku*; high-quality *washi* paper from Nara. As the quality of these materials decreases, the Ishiis' work is affected. Part of the pleasure has been knowing some of Japan's foremost artists, as they do mounting for the best-known art group in Japan, called Nitten. In the past when Hiroyoshi was still an apprentice, artists sometimes came to work in the Ishiis' factory. Hiroyoshi shares an embarrassing secret with Shiko Munakata, an artist of international fame. Munakata had asked Hiroyoshi where the handle indentation was to be put on a *fusuma* he was painting. Hiroyoshi pointed to the wrong place and Munakata marked it with a circle so as not to paint on this space. Hiroyoshi is probably the only one who knows the meaning of this circle today; it quietly sits among a lot of brush strokes on a *fusuma* in Tokyo Honganji temple in Asakusa.

Is Mr. Ishii's son going to follow in the family's footsteps? "He's in university right now," replies Hiroyoshi Ishii. "I don't suspect he really wants to join us. I know I didn't. But a long tradition like this gives us a feeling of responsibility." Hiroyoshi entered the family business even though he had wanted to be a photographer, and his father had wanted to be a scholar. "It's the fate of the oldest son of a family in a country like ours."

Local Laborers

The work of the *tobishoku*, or local laborer, like all construction-related work, has increased enormously due to the construction boom. If anything, they're too busy, says Katsumi Nakano, an independent *tobishoku* who lives and works in Asakusa. Large construction firms are flooded with so much work that they don't have an adequate supply of laborers. But even before this boom, Mr. Nakano kept quite busy thanks to solid connections with his neighborhood association group (*chonai-kai*). Independent workers retaining the traditional relationship with their community, a relationship full of give-and-take and communication, are becoming fewer and fewer in this increasingly compartmentalized age.

Tobishoku "salarymen" have come into being, workers who have traded independence and local contacts for secure jobs. Many of today's *tobishoku* have graduated from the Tokyo Metropolitan Kogyo Gakko, a two-year training course that is taken after completing ninth grade. Then they enter a large construction firm and work until retirement.

This is not the way things have always been, though. Mr. Nakano is a man whose livelihood depends on his participation in all sorts of local activities that are seemingly unrelated to the work of a *tobishoku*. He and his cronies form a living institution that is essential to the social functions of their community.

Since Mr. Nakano started his work forty-five years ago at the age of sixteen, a few things have changed. Building frames are often made of metal now, but apart from the difference in materials he is still preparing the ground and assembling the frames of buildings as he always has. He puts the pieces together, often balancing without supports on top of a beam five or six stories high. His *shichibu* pants fit tight against his calves and billow out from the knee to enable free movement. Usually of a gray or navy color, they are said to have been designed after Western riding pants. The black *jikatabi* (split-toed rubber-soled footwear) on his feet help

him keep his balance. His helmet is a more recent part of his work uniform, and the *hanten*, due to its floppy sleeves, is no longer worn on the job.

Like the *tobishoku* of the Edo Period, he is an active participant at all local events. Preparations for New Year's, in particular, are the local *tobishoku's* domain. They hang neighborhood decorations, help with preparations at shrines and participate in the ritual *mochi* making (glutinous rice pounding). They are the ones to take these decorations down, too, each with its special timing (*kadomatsu* on January 6, *kagami mochi* four days later, and large bamboo displays five days after that) and separate them into their simple elements before they are thrown away. Hanging lanterns, sweeping grounds, setting up stalls, giving out saké, and many other tasks related to shrine festivals are also performed by *hanten*-clad *tobishoku*. And the work is done free of charge. "We're like handymen in a way because we can do almost anything," Mr. Nakano explains. "Of course this is all community service. The large company *tobishoku* don't do any work for free, but this is our custom. It comes in handy, too, because the neighborhood association pays us back indirectly by giving us local construction work."

Mr. Nakano and Heiji Oketa are talking about their work with warm voices, confidence, and pride. We are in a charming, old-style tavern in Asakusa that Mr. Oketa built himself about twenty-one years ago. Everything is handmade out of natural materials.

JIKATABI

The ceiling is of woven mat and materials include bamboo, stone, paper, and various kinds of wood. These men are real talkers with broad easygoing attitudes, men who can get along with almost anyone. When asked what the difficult side of his work is, Mr. Nakano says it is his community responsibilities. "If a neighbor dies suddenly, for instance, I will have to stop whatever paid work I'm doing and go pitch in with the funeral preparations—setting up tents, arranging flower displays, and helping out. This gets in the way of making a living," he shrugs, "but it's a sad and difficult time for someone. It's not so bad to be the one to lend a hand, I guess."

What's the best part of your work? "The festivals," says Mr. Oketa. "To put on my *hanten* and take part, the panache of it all. Now that's the best part." On a wall is a large picture of a *mikoshi* (portable shrine) being paraded through the streets of Asakusa on the shoulders of thirty or more men. On top of the *mikoshi* in snappy festival garb is Mr. Oketa, fan in hand, chanting and directing the group.

"It's a good feeling to be a community figure," Mr. Nakano adds. "We are part of almost everything that happens here, we are involved. It's a nice warm feeling. You know, the salaryman type isn't really Japanese. A real Japanese has a role in his neighborhood—he's a human first and last. At least that's how it's always been here in *shitamachi*."

Handmade Paper

The invention of paper, like the invention of the wheel, was a gigantic leap in development that changed the world. The spread of information, beginning with the education of the masses and the cheap reproduction of books and journals, was instrumental to progress. Poised on the edge of what Alvin Toffler calls "the third wave"—the end of the industrial age and beginning of a new decentralized age—we may witness a future that is no longer reliant on paper, one in which information is recorded, stored, and transmitted by computer, bypassing paper altogether.

All paper, whether manufactured or handmade, is made in basically the same way. Cellulose fibers of plants or trees are treated and mixed in water. This mixture is poured on mesh screens, the water drains off, and the fibers mat to form a sheet. The sheet is removed from the screen, then pressed and dried.

There are two methods of accumulating fibers on a screen: the *tamezuki* (collecting) method from China which is used worldwide, and the *nagashizuki* (straining) method which is unique to Japan. In this latter method, mucilage from *tororo-aoi* (Hibiscus manihot) or *noriutsugi* (Hydrangea paniculta) plants is added in order to suspend the fibers, thicken the mixture, and delay the draining time. This allows optimum control over paper thickness

and fiber alignment. Water is cast out over the frame, more mixture is added, and water is cast again repeatedly. This achieves the interlocking alignment of fibers that provides the strength of *washi*.

Yokichi Uchino is a seventh-generation *washi* maker from Ogawamachi, Saitama Prefecture. He cultivates rice, but paper-making provides about 80 percent of his income. He says *washi* use is on the rise due to increased affluence and leisure time. The number of traditional *washi* makers, however, has decreased. After the war there were about 600 in Ogawamachi alone. Competition was stiff, dealers squeezed the makers, and many converted to machines. Today there are only eighteen families making *washi* in his town.

Less competition and increased use have made *washi* a rather attractive business. Nevertheless, few children want to succeed their parents in the trade. This lack of interest on the part of Japanese youth is perhaps offset by the pride of having foreigners come to learn *washi* making. Mr. Uchino taught a Spaniard for about a year, and receives samples from Spain for advice and comment.

Of its various uses over the ages—in documents, sutras, woodblock prints, *fusuma*, shoji—the military uses of *washi* were perhaps the most unusual: in former days it was used to seal the joints of samurai armor, and during the Second World War it was used as a substitute for leather and for balloons to carry bombs in a last-ditch (and unsuccessful) plan to bomb the United States.

What is the difference between *washi* and the paper used for newspapers? If you clip out a newspaper article and save it, it will turn yellow and eventually disintegrate. Newspaper is made of ground wood pulp which is not durable. While wood pulp is added to the cheaper range of papers in Japan, good *washi* is made from the fibers of special bushes, is tear- and insect-resistant, and can last for hundreds of years. Fine grades of Western paper use cellulose from cloth or linen for the main ingredient; Japanese *washi* uses the cellulose of four plants. It is classified according to material: *mashi* made of hemp, *kozoshi* of mulberry, *mitsumata* of E*dgeworthia papyrifera*, and *ganpishi* of D*iplomorpha sikokiana*.

One can judge the quality of *washi* by tearing it and examining the fibers. Paper that is easy to tear has little fiber. The more fiber in the paper, the better the quality. There is a distinctive smooth glaze to 100 percent mulberry paper, which is among the best-quality *washi*.

In the past, paper consumption per person was a reliable index to the standard of living in a country. The better the lifestyle, the more paper used. The futuristic "paperless office" may change this. Today, one wonders if silicon chips and floppy disks are not the true indicators of wealth in lifestyles. In any case, Mr. Uchino can feel secure that even if machine-made paper declines in usefulness, his *washi*, a product for leisure that is inextricably connected with Japanese culture, will neither disintegrate nor fade away.

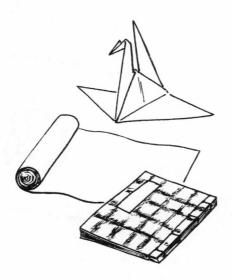

Votive Plaques

Want to pass that crucial exam, make a big sale, or recover from a serious illness? If so, what you need is an *ema* (votive plaque). These wooden tablets have been a common cure-all in Japan since as far back as A.D. 736. Today they can still be seen at most temples and Shinto shrines—desperate pleas to the pantheon of Japanese gods—dangling from various structures and rattling against each other in the wind.

Ancient shrines used to keep live horses for ceremonial purposes—to quell epidemics, for example, or to reduce or increase rain according to agricultural needs. The horse served as a vehicle for various gods and as a messenger between this world and the next. Gradually, however, the expense of acquiring and maintaining these animals became prohibitive for ordinary shrines, and paintings executed on flat wooden surfaces called *ema* were created as a modest substitute. The word itself explains its origin: the *e* character means picture and *ma*, a horse.

Initially, three-dimensional wooden statues were created to substitute for the live horses. It was thought until recently that these statues gradually developed into free-standing flat boards during the Muromachi (1336–1568) and Edo periods. However, a wooden *ema* made of Japanese cypress was discovered in 1989 at the Nara ruins of Heijokyo, the Nara Period (710–94) Japanese

capital, in the remains of the palace of Nagaya-o (grandson of Emperor Temmu). It depicts a red and white horse carrying an ornamental saddle. Dating back to 736, it is thought to have been offered to eliminate the smallpox epidemic of 735.

With time, the subjects depicted on the these tablets multi-plied. By the end of the Edo Period there were specific *ema* for most circumstances and aspirations. The horse ones remained as "all-purpose" *ema*, but the majority depicted a theme or motif relating to a deity or symbol, often related to specific shrines or temples.

For instance, the pomegranate and peach express a wish for progeny; a lock indicates the determination to give up a bad habit (smoking, drinking, gambling, or sexual obsessions); black bulls are for learning; a couple facing away from each other is a wish to end a marriage. Curative varieties include the catfish for relief from skin disorders and the octopus to cure warts.

Previously, the design of the *ema* itself was sufficient, but it has gradually become the custom to write one's explicit wishes and name right on the *ema* itself. Even today, down-to-earth "education mamas" send their kids to cram school and offer *ema* to shrines to help them pass entrance exams. In fact, *ema* can be seen as a type of barometer for current social problems and concerns. E*ma* hanging at Tokyo's Nezu Shrine are mostly the usual exam and health pleas. Among them, however, is "please let me grow taller than 145 centimeters," written by a young girl. Another is a plea to win the lottery for new public housing. A "thank you" was added later for having won.

Choko Yoshida is living in an old, handsome wooden building in Kita Senju. She is an eighth-generation *ema* maker, having taken over when her father died ten years ago. She is continuing the family tradition because she is the eldest of five daughters—there are no sons in the family. Machine-made *ema* are being produced in profusion these days, but hand-nailed, hand-painted ones are made by, at most, only a handful of people.

Mrs. Yoshida uses thinly cut Japanese cedar, which she nails to a cedar frame. She paints traditional designs, but because different people have different styles, her *ema* can be distinguished from her father's by the brush strokes. She paints fifteen distinct designs and, altogether, about two thousand a year now. "Customers are thinning out," she says, "but still, people living around here buy them every year to keep around their homes. I have two types of customers now: faithful customers from way back and *ema* collectors. A lot of collectors come here because a hand-painted *ema* is quite unusual these days."

"Tell, me," I ask, "do they really have any effect, these votive offerings?"

"They do, don't you think? Otherwise people wouldn't buy them, now, would they."

Left: "Please let grandfather get well."
Right: "Help me pass my university entrance exams."

Festivals and Events

Spaced Out at Ueno

You'll need a sleeping bag and a tent if you want to celebrate under the cherry blossoms at Ueno Park. Of all the things that are precious in this nation, space is at the top of the list. And the ultimate in high-priority space has got to be the few hundred meters under Ueno's famous cherry trees during the seven days of official "cherry blossom viewing" in April.

The custom of *hanami*, or "flower viewing," is probably derived from the ancient agricultural practice of picnicking in the fields and hills during the religious festivals that marked the beginning of spring and the planting of new crops. Aristocratic flower-viewing parties are recorded as far back as the Heian Period (794–1185), and Toyotomi Hideyoshi threw some extravagant parties during the Momoyama Period (1568–1603) at Kyoto's Daigoji temple. By the Edo Period (1603–1868) even the common people had taken to eating, drinking saké, singing songs, and dancing under the blooming cherry trees.

Cherry blossom viewing has not only secured a prominent place in Japanese literature, theater, dance, and the fine arts, but it has stubbornly clung to the hearts of even the trendiest Japanese. Unlike so many other of Japan's old customs, the popularity of *hanami* has, if

anything, increased with industrialization and modernization. There is a saying, *hana yori dango*, a slightly sardonic comment that the food is of more interest than the blooming flowers. Perhaps this is the secret of the longevity of *hanami*. Or perhaps it's the freedom to drink from dawn to dusk on these seven special days. Or the brief respite from the daily grind. Whatever it is, there seems to be no age barrier or generation gap involved. In fact, at the end of March and in early April, radio and television stations broadcast hourly reports on the condition of local cherry trees, following the progress of their blooming from southern Kyushu all the way to Wakkanai in northernmost Hokkaido.

Part of any self-respecting company's spring offensive includes at least one large bash under the boughs, and in a city as prestige-conscious as Tokyo, Ueno is a prime and traditional target. Planning is left to the *kakari* (person in charge) but the real nitty-gritty duty of fighting for the turf is usually relegated to the company *kohai*, the lowest-ranking employees on the totem poll. These "new faces" (newly recruited freshmen) are called on to show their mettle.

Imagine my surprise last year when I found Ueno Park teeming with activity one fine April morning during my usual 6:00 A.M. run. Blue plastic tarps were spread out everywhere with bodies strewn over them like bugs stuck on flypaper—an occasional sleeping bag, futon, rocking chair, or plastic chaise longue attached. And a swarm of corporate soldiers armed with rope and more tarpaulins were rushing here and there trying to stake out new territory. It was only after hearing TV interviews that I realized that many of these courageous young men were having their first overnight camping experience right here in Ueno Park, all in the line of duty.

The way things are escalating I wouldn't be at all surprised if people started camping out a week ahead of time in order to get the best possible spots.

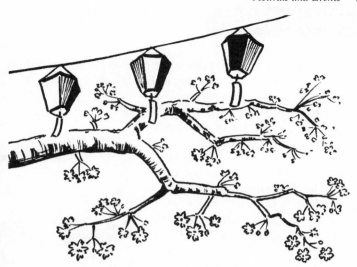

Glory in the Flower

For many Japanese, summer does not officially start until they make a trip to Tokyo's Iriya Market to buy morning glories. The Iriya Market is in full swing every year for three days from around July 6, in its traditional place in front of Kishibojin temple, just east of Ueno Park.

Invariably marked by a crowd and colorful, loud merchants calling out their wares under makeshift bamboo lean-tos, the scene is lit by blindingly white light bulbs interspersed with handmade paper lanterns adorned with morning glories and shop names in thick black *sumi* ink strokes. Despite the haggling sounds and the merchants' cries and the bustle of purchases, the prices of the flowers are fixed; everyone is selling their goods at uniform prices. Yet it looks like a bargain sale with its milling crowds, TV crews, and festive atmosphere.

Iriya was a district of paddy fields until the late Meiji Era (1868–1912), and one could look across the paddies to Yoshiwara (red-light district) and its villas. The last morning-glory nurseries disappeared from Iriya in 1912. Today plants are trucked in from the northern and eastern outskirts of Tokyo.

And what a selection! Reds, pinks, purples, blues; Western, Japanese, and Korean morning glories, ranging in price from 700 to about 2,000 yen. One of the hottest-selling varieties recently was the Danjuro, a tannish flower described in Japanese as "shrimp-tea" (*ebi cha*) color. The Danjuro is named after the famous Kabuki actor of the same name and its color is said to be that of his family crest. (I searched for a Kikugoro or a Shikan glory to no avail.) The Korean glories also

caught my eye—lacy delicate leaves and a flower about the size of a one-yen coin.

The vendors, who add as much color to the festival as the morning glories themselves, are a varied group. Some are actual farmers, some own flower shops, some are professional festival men who work in the *yomise* (night shops) that line up around local festivals, and some are students. What they have in common is their costume—tight-fitting indigo pants and shirts in all manner of traditional patterns, covered by a *haragake*, a kind of dark blue apron slung in front which has a kangaroo pocket for money, receipts, or whatever might be useful to have on hand. Around their foreheads thin towels or indigo-print cloths are tied in various jaunty fashions. Feet sport thongs, black split-toed *jikatabi*, geta, and even high-heeled sandals on some young men. They shout, they posture, they give detailed explanations. Just watching them in action is entertaining.

There are about sixty official stalls at the Iriya Market as well as

countless unofficial shops along the back streets. Official shops have location "rights" along the road in front of Kishibojin temple that, for the most part, were bought about forty years ago when the market was revived. I was told that they are charged about 10,000 yen for electricity, and a nominal rent. Shops in the best locations sell 2,500 pots or more over the three days they are open.

The *yukata*, as much a symbol of summer as the morning glories are, is seen at Iriya each year. Young marriageable ladies venture forth in *yukata* and *cho-cho* (butterfly-shaped) obi for their ritual purchase, a festive yearly outing. Older women and men also join in the bustling sartorial parade, stopping at Kishibojin temple for a prayer and some trinkets. This year, along with a handful of old women and men, only a few young beauties posed for cameras and rather self-consciously made the rounds in the traditional cotton kimono. Let's hope that the *yukata*, recently popular wear for summer dates, will also make a comeback at the Iriya Market.

Dancing in the Street

Just as the Iriya morning-glory festival marks the beginning of summer in Tokyo, *bon odori*, or summer dancing, marks the end.

Outdoor local dances, once a part of all communities in Japan, date back at least to the fifteenth century, and perhaps as far back as the Buddhist folk dances (*odori nenbutsu*) of the late Heian Period.

At the end of August, Tokyo's *shitamachi* area is alive with street dancing in the hot evenings. Individual blocks or larger areas organize these affairs. The general mood is set by drums beating a tribal rhythm and by little kids winging about in colorful *yukata* with their hair done up in fancy pins, eating cotton candy and drinking *ramune* (a sweet soft drink in a bottle with a glass ball stopper). Oval *uchiwa* fans flutter and *yukata*—lots of them, many of the same pattern and coloring—are seen everywhere. These *yukata* are ordered every other year by each area, which chooses its own specific design.

People from certain areas can be identified not only by their *yukata* patterns, but also by their particular way of dancing. In Tokyo, anyway, most areas dance the same basic dances—*Tokyo Ondo*, *Tanko Bushi*, *Obakyu*, and others—but each local group develops slight variations. Thus, one can identify those who have clogged over from neighboring streets as being from somewhere else. Dancing is done in a circle usually around a *yagura*, or temporary platform upon which the older and more skillful dancers perform under brightly lit lanterns, serving as models for the rest of the crowd.

Before participating, one wraps a few thousand-yen notes in a

piece of paper, and writes the amount and one's name on it, preferably in brush calligraphy. This is proffered to the *chonai-kai*, the neighborhood elders, who preside in an emptied storefront among bottles of donated saké and decorations. A token is given in return. Last year I received a *hachimaki* (headband) with my district's name, Majima-cho, on it, and some chits for soft drinks.

One's name and donation amount is immediately listed up on a huge board, for all to see. I am told that it is not good to give too much or too little. Check the board ahead of time to see what one's neighbors and peers are giving.

Lured by the drums, everyone is out either watching or joining in. The music, other than the drums which are beat with macho flourish by local boys and men, is played off an old phonograph. Selections are made and announced by the head of the *chonai-kai* who quite often has a bottle of saké in one hand and a *karaoke* microphone in the other.

Mixed with the loud music are boisterous greetings, laughter, and gossip. This is a tradition that is as fundamental to the socialization of our area as the public bath. It is one that seems to be fading away. Of course, "official" *bon odori* dancers will continue to appear at special occasions to show the uninitiated the cultural traditions linked with ancestral worship and the agricultural past. But the tradition and intimacy of everyday people dancing in their neighborhoods year after year as a social event seems to be ebbing. The building boom is interfering, for one thing. Our new neighbors in their condominium apartments rarely venture forth to the local "hot spots" (e.g., the public bath and festivals) where we all congregate and socialize. And as individual families are forced to move out of the area, the number of dancers is likewise thinning out.

One important thing: *bon odori* is nothing spectacular to watch. This is why preserving it just to demonstrate it as a former custom loses much of its meaning. The fun, the excitement, the socialization is in the dancing, moving to the beat of the drums, wearing your *yukata* in the summer heat, surrounded by friends and neighbors. I know a lot of people who don't like *bon odori* who have never participated in it. But anyone who tries it once, loves it—the mood is infectious. At the end of August there are dances here and there all over *shitamachi*. But if you come, don't just watch. Put on a *yukata*, get behind one of the old ladies, and try it for yourself.

Raking in the Money

Take a look at the walls of your local shops and eateries. There is probably an ornamental rake—covered with pine needles, cherry blossoms, golden coins, rice baskets, cranes, turtles, the seven gods of luck, and perhaps a pudgy white smiling face—hanging in one corner. This decorative rake, the *kumade*, is as indispensable an object to any sushi, eel, or noodle shop, nightclub, grocery, or bookstore as the ubiquitous welcoming cat. After the cat welcomes a customer in, the rake helps pull in his money.

Tokyoites who want to have a financially successful year will visit the Otori Festival in November to trade in last year's rake for one that is a little bigger, a bit more ornate, and anywhere from a little to a lot more expensive.

During this time, the Otori Shrine precinct is invaded by school girls, Ginza hostesses, vaudeville actors, Kabuki stars, day laborers, and businessmen. People gawk, admire, and barter, while others eat and drink along the path inside the usually silent shrine. By the time you get to the area containing the stalls selling the rakes, you are being swept around by the crowds and dazzled by the spectacle.

Color and tinsel glitter down from the heights of large, deep stalls. Rake styles differ markedly from one stall to the next, some ornate, some simple, and some outrageous. The largest stalls display gargantuan designs with the names of their famous patrons dangling from them. This means of showing off insures that a crowd will be hanging around for a glimpse of Kankuro or some other famous actor when he comes to pick up his

order. Sellers prance and call out their wares. The best of them keep a monologue going and work the crowd. Once a sale is made, the shop's entire staff gathers to join in the 3–3–3–1 clap and shout "Banzai!" Late in the evening, it's not uncommon for a large bottle of saké to be uncorked and shared.

At last year's Otori Festival, Keiko Yoshida stood quietly warming her hands at a charcoal-filled hibachi inside her stall while around her the hubbub of the chattering and pushing crowds careened and swirled, and less successful shopkeepers screamed our their wares under glaring light bulbs. A red "Beware of Fires" ribbon was slung across her kimono and her beehive hairdo was immaculately in place. Four of her helpers in indigo coats and colorful twisted headbands had foreheads reddened from the contents of a bottle kept almost, but not completely, out of sight on the ground.

In contrast to Mrs. Yoshida's serene expression, their faces beamed with joy. They had sold all of her rakes—not only at this centrally located stall, but at two others wedged down side rows among the hundreds of competing establishments. It was only 8:00 P.M., and this had never happened before in anyone's memory. "We've really raked it in this year," one joked. Everyone roared with laughter, despite the bad pun.

The triumph was Mrs. Yoshida's, who has been making the rakes for over forty years. Her husband's grandfather had started the business in the early Meiji Era. Since then, they have won a large and loyal following of customers who call in special orders every October.

Her designs are those created by her husband and his grandfather, and her materials are all natural—cardboard, wood, and bamboo. Each little piece of cardboard is hand painted and assembled. Last year they had made about one thousand elaborate rakes in her home right around the corner from the shrine. Her prices range from 5,000 to 200,000 yen.

When asked if she thought women have gotten stronger recently, Mrs. Yoshida thought for a moment and shook her head.

"No," she said firmly. "The men have gotten weak. And they've changed. The E*dokko* (male resident of Tokyo's *shitamachi*) had panache. He would haggle about the price of a rake shamelessly. We'd finally sell it to him for five yen. After he paid this, he would proudly toss down the original full price as a tip. There aren't many with that kind of strong character now."

KUMADE

Seasonal Customs

Seasonal Markers

The sounds of summer include the tinkling of wind chimes; the throbbing whine of cicadas; the caged *suzumushi*, a bug with a bell-like cry, reminding us that cooler days are on the way; the click-clack of wooden geta on pavement. Over the past two millennia, the heavy, humid heat of Japan has inspired ingenious methods of luring one's attention away from the dreadful discomfort. But since air conditioners hit the market in 1955, a multitude of summer traditions have been fast disappearing.

Thanks to air conditioning, hot days are certainly more comfortable but summer is becoming just another division of the calendar, unpunctuated by the seasonal flourishes and trimmings that were once a vital part of this agricultural nation. The flavor and special aura of summer have slipped away. As we sit comfortably in our cool homes, watching TV, drinking Cokes, and munching on potato chips, we may not notice that our seasonal markers have all but disappeared.

The musky smoke from pressed green coils of a mosquito repellent called *katorisenko*, traditionally burnt in ceramic pig-shaped containers, is perhaps the most recognizable smell of Japanese summer. The insecticide itself was developed from a plant called pyrethrum (a type of chrysanthemum) that was introduced to Japan by Americans in 1885; the stylish coil shape was designed in Japan. Other summery smells include the special scent of the yellow flower called *tsukimiso* which blooms at night, and the heavy stench of firecrackers.

Oval fish bowls with goldfish gliding within and large blocks of ice set out on tables to melt are some of the ingenious visual methods that refresh by suggestion. The mere sight of summer sweets such as *kuzu zakura* with its see-through envelope is calculated to cool one down, as are transparent foods like *tokoroten*, clear noodles made of agar, which were cooling people off as far back as the Nara Period (710–94). Crushed ice, *kakigori*, dates back to the Heian Period (794–1185), when ice was painstakingly preserved throughout the hot summers.

The highly touted "cool" wooden Japanese-style homes often feel like ovens in the summer, a feature which has traditionally enticed people outside in the evenings to cool off. Men in white underwear called *suteteko*—baggy pants extending below the knees and T-shirts with half sleeves—sometimes with towels folded on their heads, sit on stools outside their homes, fanning themselves with large oval *uchiwa* fans and talking to passersby. In the past they sat on light cool bamboo benches called *endai* and played *shogi*, a game similar to chess, a *katorisenko* pig at their feet belching out its mosquito killer. Both women and men donned cotton *yukata*, cool summer kimono, the hems of which the men often folded up into their obi to expose their legs to the breeze.

The doors of homes were slid open and covered by *sudare*, or straw blinds, providing communication between those within and without. A tatami room illuminated by an exposed light bulb with the hot inhabitants at a low table covered with beer bottles and glasses, the TV droning, and an old electric fan with attached cloth or plastic strings dancing frantically in its wind is a common sight even today in places like Tokyo's *shitamachi*.

Mosquito netting, *kaya*, made of linen and strung up on hooks at each corner of a room before sleeping, was considered indispensable before the war. Some families put fireflies in the nets to delight their children. Folding the *kaya* in the morning was an arduous task that many elderly Japanese still remember fondly.

Combating the oppressive heat was part of the motivation behind the summer festivals and the evening street dancing. And many people remember jumping into the Sumida River from bridges and swimming in it as well. Boats with roofs on them for evening entertainment (*yakatabune*), popular with Heian Period court people, are still used on the Sumida River.

Since 1733, the July "opening" of the Sumida River—the first day of the year that people were allowed to enter the water—has been celebrated by fireworks (official "opening days" for swimming remain a tenacious custom throughout Japan). Smaller *senko hanabi* (sparklers) and *nezumi* firecrackers so named because they skit around in circles like rats are still prized by children.

Outdoor bathing in tubs surrounded by *amado* panels; *obon* customs including the eggplant and cucumber animals to transport ghostly spirits home and back; flypaper coiling down from ceilings; electric fans with strings tied to them dancing in the heat; *ramune*; *mugicha* (cold barley tea); watermelon; watering down streets in the morning and evening; grilling fish outside over *sumi* charcoal—the unique rituals of summer are fading away: people now tend to stay in their cooled houses rather than going outside to chat in the evenings. Year-round food and drinks are replacing the seasonal ones, and insects are under control. As my seventy-nine-year-old neighbor puts it, "It sure is more comfortable. But not very much fun."

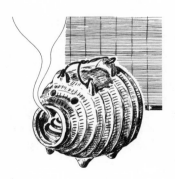

Natural Ice

There's nothing like a refreshing dish of flavored crushed ice to cool you off on hot summer days. A square white cloth emblazoned with a red or blue kanji character for ice still hangs in front of many shops in the summer, indicating that they sell chipped ice topped with strawberry, lemon, or melon syrup. Eating *kakigori*, this crushed ice, has been a national pleasure for centuries. But, when you're outside dripping with sweat in the oppressive heat, have you ever wondered where that ice came from, the ice that cooled the emperor off in the summers of, say, the Heian Period?

Were they hiding freezers in their castles? The answer, of course, is no. But they were using ice. Ice made from water that was naturally frozen in the middle of winter and carefully preserved through the hot months of summer in Heian Period storehouses called *himuro*. Up to two-thirds of the ice would melt before the end of summer, leaving a precious third for the enjoyment of the court people. By the Edo Period (1603–1868), many local lords owned their own ice-storage rooms, and the demand for ice increased so much by the Meiji Era (1868–1912) that its artificial production started to rival that of natural ice.

If you travel to the mountains of Chichibu in the winter, you may be able to get a peek at what ice production was like in centuries past. Yoshio Asami is still harvesting thick blocks (70 by 50 by 15 centimeters each) of natural ice every winter in much the same way as three generations of his family have for over a century. The mountains surrounding the Chichibu area make it ideal for natural ice. Winter days here are clear, the air is dry, and the lowest temperatures at night are often lower than those of northern Honshu.

Natural ice is called *tennengori* and is still used for crushed ice sweets as well as in combination with whiskey at select drinking establishments. Its medical use to lower fever has ended, and Mr. Asami says there are only a few places in Japan that still harvest it.

As a result the use of *tennengori* is dwindling to almost nothing.

Mr. Asami has filled three large ponds (132, 198, and 264 square meters) each December for the past fifty years. In a good year he works from December 15 until about February 10. Once the ponds are filled it takes two weeks of minus six- to minus seven-degree weather to freeze water to a thickness of fifteen centimeters. At that point the tedious process of sawing the ice begins. Until

about 1990, they did all the sawing by hand and it took one and a half months to cut his three ponds. The job is now done in about one and a half days with an electric saw.

Although cutting the actual blocks has become easier, other hardships remain. During the freezing season he must cut the edges of his ponds every morning before 6:00 A.M. Failure to do so would cause the concrete basins to crack. On early dark mornings that are bitterly cold, even his yearly nine months of vacation seem an inadequate reward for the effort.

The mountain water must be filtered and Mr. Asami has had to build facilities to avoid sunlight and eliminate dust. His six workers wear special clean boots and gloves, and great efforts are taken to keep the ice clean while it is being tended to and cut. Even so, an occasional particle remains. Fancy hotels, including one of the best in Tokyo, in fact, ordered ice from Asami for a while. It was thought that natural ice would add an elegant, high-class appeal for whiskey drinkers. However, worried by complaints

from a fastidious customer, they decided that less exotic but totally particle-free ice would be safer and ceased using *tennengori*.

Recently fewer people have been eating Mr. Asami's ice because of Japan's unseasonably warm winters. In good years he has collected as many as five batches of ice. But in l992, the first (and only) batch was collected on January 24, ten days later than the year before. Overall weather conditions are getting warmer, he frets. And even with the aid of an electric saw, the future of *tennengori* in Chichibu is in jeopardy. At sixty-five, Mr. Asami says he is running out of steam, yet there isn't anyone to take his place. His son just shook his head when we asked the prospects of his taking over. "It's not much of a living that you can make these days; most people want a better lifestyle."

His father listened to this with an expressionless face, perhaps recalling wonderful summers spent in the nearby swimming hole, fishing, playing his saxophone, and making some 360 *shakuhachi* (bamboo flutes) by hand in his spare time. A man of many interests and talents, Mr. Asami has nine months to indulge himself in them. He develops his own photographs and was the first in Chichibu to take color photos. Sitting out on the sunny porch, he seemed a picture of contentment, one of the few who has lived a productive life of leisure, even while earning his living by holding down a trade.

Fire Watches

It's cold in the winter, and those of us living in traditional Japanese fashion make special efforts to keep warm. The wooden houses and *nagaya* (row houses) were built with summer in mind, with the idea of letting the breeze in and the humidity (and accompanying mold) out. So in the winter we sip tea and huddle half under the *kotatsu*, the heated low table, in warm cotton padded jackets. The *kotatsu* and hibachi are our only heat.

In the evenings I lay out the bedding before we go to the nearby public bath. After soaking in the piping-hot water (up to 46 degrees Celsius), we hurry back and dive into the futon before we cool off. If too much time elapses between bath and bed, it is difficult to warm up. This living with the elements, feeling the change of seasons, is Spartan but in some ways utterly luxurious. As we lie in the thick layers of our futon, we close our eyes and concentrate on the sounds around us.

The muffled movements of the neighbors preparing for bed can be heard through the walls. A cat has jumped onto the clay-tiled roof with a thud and is making its way along the gutter. The refrigerator hum stops suddenly with a rusty-sounding clunk. Then, from off in the distance, the resounding ring of

wooden clappers being struck twice and a deep musical voice calling *"hi no yo-jin, hi no yo-jin"* (beware of fires) wafts toward us. After a short pause the clappers are heard again, a little closer, and the call is repeated. The clappers have the crisp, high-pitched sound that only oak can make. It's the same noise that heralds the curtain opening at Kabuki and is also used to heighten suspense at crucial points in the drama. But outside in the cold dark air, it rebounds off the wooden houses and tiled roofs of the area with a lonely, almost eerie effect.

Winter in Tokyo is cold, windy, and dry—nearly perfect conditions for conflagration. Indeed, vast sections of the city burned down in the past, as in the fires of 1657, 1772, and 1829 during the Edo Period. Because of this, *"hi no yojin"* has been called out on winter evenings in Tokyo since that time. In those days the system, then called *jishinban*, was a combination of fire warning and police vigilance. There was a *jishinban* with its own fire tower every two or three blocks and manning it was a paying job.

Today in my area there are forty-four men who take part in calling out the warnings, two at a time, from December 22 through the end of February, on a volunteer basis. One holds a lantern in one hand and a flashlight in the other, and the second man strikes the wooden clappers and calls out. The men are between thirty and fifty years old and they go out at 10:00 P.M. and make the rounds for anywhere from thirty to ninety minutes.

Of course, nowadays modern buildings have central heating and their tenants don't have to bother with turning the heat on and off. And the newer buildings and houses have thick walls so you can't hear street calls anyway. The ritual of *hi no yojin* is a leftover from the Edo Period that has all but died out. But in Tokyo's Yanaka-Nezu area, one of the few remaining holdouts of old wooden buildings, there is still a need. In fact, nowadays, there is a waiting list for potential *hi no yojin* callers; more neighbors want to participate in this ritual than are needed. Perhaps it's because this is the last vestige of the "good life" here in *shitamachi*:

of community, of season, of belonging to your environment and neighborhood in a natural way.

"Hi *no yo-jin, hi no yo-jin*," the call is becoming louder and louder. "Ah, isn't that the voice of our neighbor, Mr. Saito?" I wonder, and drift off to sleep.

Homemade Osechi Ryori

Osechi ryori (New Year's dishes) originally comprised food made for five ceremonies called go-sekku that were imported from China during the Nara Period (710–94). Today, however, osechi ryori is connected exclusively with the New Year. It is closely related to seasonal decorations, such as the horaikazari in which rice (kome), rice cakes (omochi), seaweed (kobu), kumquats (kinkan), bitter oranges (daidai), chestnuts (kuri), spiny lobsters (Ise ebi), herring roe (kazunoko), dried anchovies (gomame), black soybeans (kuromame), and radishes (daikon) are placed along with other things on a wooden stand as a New Year's offering to the gods for a good harvest and prosperity.

Traditionally put in lacquer boxes called jubako that are stacked on top of each other, osechi ryori is to be eaten over a period of three days. Since food was limited during the winter to plant roots, dried, and preserved foods, osechi ryori was prepared before New Year's Eve to provide a three-day respite from cooking. It facilitates the tradition not to do any work involving water (e.g., cooking and washing) for the first three days of the year.

In the Edo Period, when the go-sekku were first celebrated by commoners, osechi ryori was served in four boxes: In Edo (old Tokyo) the top box contained herring eggs, black beans, and dried anchovies; the second, food to be served with saké or tea at the beginning of a meal, such as mashed chestnuts (kinton), rolled cooked egg (datemaki), and fish cake (kamaboko); the third, food from the sea and rivers, such as rolled kelp (kobumaki), grilled fish (yakizakana) and sweet-boiled fish (kanroni); and the bottom box contained vegetables, such as devil's tongue (konnyaku), burdock (gobo) and lotus root (renkon). Today's osechi ryori retains its good luck or engi meanings and bursts with symbolism.

For those of you who want to know what sort of symbols and meanings you may ingest, here is a list of the most common: kazunoko—many children; kuromame—labor and health (the color of a tanned laborer); *gomame*—good harvest; *kinton*—"*kin*" means gold, i.e. wealth; *kobu*—reference to "*yorokobu*" meaning luck; *tai* (sea bream)—reference to "*medetai*" meaning congratulatory; *datemaki*—"*maku*," to roll, indicates scrolls, the development of literature and culture; red and white *kamaboko*—the colors mean peace; *renkon*—the holes symbolize seeing into the future; *daidai*— "*dai*" means generation and twice indicates continuity of the family line; I*se ebi* (or spiny lobster)—the bent back suggests elderly people and thus a long life; *omochi*—play on "*mochi*" meaning long lasting, or long life; *toshi-koshi soba* (year-crossing noodles,

eaten on New Year's Eve)—long noodles symbolize long lives, continuity and the lengthening of family fortunes.

Until thirty some years ago, all *osechi ryori* was prepared at home. Kazuo Nakazato, floor manager for a Tokyu Department Store's food department, reports that although boxed *osechi ryori* was first put on the market around 1970, for at least ten years before that they had sold various kinds of *osechi ryori* separately at their food counters. Sales of their pre-ordered *osechi ryori* boxes have been increasing by about 10 percent each year. There are four types being sold now—traditional, Western, Chinese, and mixed. Prices range from 13,000 to 100,000 yen with the average box at 20,000 yen. These pre-ordered feasts are prepared by specialty restaurants, including *kaiseki* restaurants for the Japanese-style boxes and well-known hotels for the Western-style meals. However, sales of traditional boxes are falling off in favor of the other types.

Even though his store's sales are steadily increasing, Mr. Nakazato believes that consumption of traditional New Year's food is on the decrease. He explains that in the past, *osechi ryori* was considered gourmet food, a real treat and a break from lackluster everyday food. As a result of Japan's prosperity, however, exotic and tasty food can be eaten anytime. *Osechi ryori* is beginning to be looked upon as "traditional" as opposed to delicious. His own family has *osechi ryori* on the first day of the New Year, but usually has meat or something entirely different that night and on the following days.

Our elderly next-door neighbor said that she will not make *osechi ryori* anymore. Her son and grandchildren don't want to eat it. A few other neighbors said they would make black and gold beans, but would also have sushi and meat (non-traditional food) along with them. Many were ordering boxes because it is not economical to make such food for four or fewer people, but only when cooking for an extended family. Women who work may not have enough time to prepare it, and young brides often don't know how. I do have one neighbor, though, who spends about five days in preparation, which includes gathering special leaves and pine needles from local parks. She produces about five trays per person of delicacies—beautiful, symbolic, and delicious—served in 100-year-old lacquerware for her ever-so-fortunate friends and family.

Dreams of Revenge

In the past, paying attention to all sorts of "firsts" of the year was a popular pastime. There was the first drawing of water (*wakamizu*), the first visit to the head of the family's home (*kadoake*), the first bath (*hatsuburo*), the first sweeping of the house (*hakizome*), and more, all with strict rules and times for observance. First dreams, or *hatsuyume*, were especially important harbingers of the future, and it was once customary to prepare ahead of time to ensure a dream that would tell one's fortune for the coming year.

According to tradition, on New Year's Eve (or the evening of the first or second—there is a curious lack of consensus among scholars, but most go for the night of January 2), street vendors would be out calling "*Otakara! Otakara!*" selling cheap woodblock prints of the seven gods of luck, the *shichifukujin*, in a boat. These prints were not made to last a long time, but rather they were to be placed under the pillow for a single night. They were the means of obtaining a lucky dream. By the next morning, the dreamer's fate for the year would be set.

The prints, called *takarabune* (treasure ship), depict a sailboat loaded with treasures and the seven lucky gods. On the sail is the character for *takara*, treasure, and somewhere around the ship is a rather peculiar palindromic poem. It tells about a long night in a boat. When everyone wakes up at dawn there is the lovely sound of waves and smooth sailing ahead.

The custom of putting a *takarabune* picture under the pillow to induce propitious dreams started for the nobility around the Muromachi Period (1336–1568). It spread to the commoners during the Edo Period where in Kansai they were sold at shrines and temples and in Edo (old Tokyo) they were sold by street vendors. In those days dreams were thought to be messages from the gods. If the dream was a bad one, it was tossed away into a river along with the print. Senrei Sekioka, a woodblock printer in Tokyo, remembers his father talking about selling the prints. Every New

Year's 200–300 prints bundled in a *furoshiki* (cloth wrapping) were taken out by vendors to sell on the streets for five sen each (probably about 250 yen today). The best place to sell these dream sheets, his father had said, was near the geisha quarters where beautiful women and their patrons often paid ten or more times the five sen hoping to "buy" good luck with a large tip.

A few vendors continued to ply dream-prints up until the Second World War. Today you can get a copy of the *takarabune* from most of the temples featuring one of the seven lucky gods (Benzaiten, Daikokuten, Ebisu, Bishamonten, Jurojin, Hotei, or Fukurokuju) or at shops such as Isetatsu that sell traditional goods. I urge you to go out and purchase one for next New Year. In the Taisho Era (1912–26), anyway, the print was considered well worth the five sen it cost.

One of my neighbors, Katsuhiro Kato, whose mother had been a hairdresser during the Meiji Era (1868–1912), remembers women tying wishes written on strips of paper onto their *kanzashi*, the decorations worn in their hair, and sticking them in their pillow along with the *takarabune*. Still others slept on pictures of the deceased, hoping to see their loved ones in their dreams. The pillows in those days were designed to protect the elaborate female coiffures and resembled wooden boxes with soft fabric on the top.

The best New Year's dream to have is one of Mount Fuji followed by one of a hawk and one of an eggplant. Among the many theories about the meanings of these dreams, the most interesting is the one connecting these symbols to the three great revenge vendettas of the Edo Period that were made popular by Kabuki theater: *Soga no Taimen*, *Kanadehon Chushingura*, and *Igagoe Dochu Sugoroku*. It was during a hunting party at Mount Fuji that the Soga brothers finally got their long-sought revenge, a story that is played at most Kabuki theaters during January. The hawk represents the Asano family's crest in the famous tale of the forty-seven samurai who avenged their lord called *Chushingura*, and the eggplant was on the family crest of Watanabe Kazuma, a main protagonist in the Araki Mataemon revenge saga *Igagoe*. In those days, one's most important desires (shows of fealty, loyalty, and honor) were often realized through revenge. I tend to credit this interpretation because, in the Edo Period, Kabuki theater was unquestionably a trendsetter for the commoners, one that greatly influenced the fashion and fads of the times. And during this same

time when *hatsuyume* became popular, these three samurai vendettas were quite the rage. The avenger's long-cherished desires
were realized; his good character and loyalty proven, hence the
connection with lucky dreams. Sweet dreams of revenge!

New Year's Fun

Japanese badminton anyone? The game of *hanetsuki* (battledore), played with elaborate paddles called *hagoita*, has been in existence since the fifteenth century, when it was played at the Imperial Court. In many ways similar to badminton, this game is traditionally reserved for females and played only during the New Year's holidays. Nowadays, one has to look long and hard to find a New Year's tourney even though the decorative paddles, the *hagoita*, are the focus of a huge, lively festival every December at Tokyo's Asakusa Kannon temple grounds.

Paddles of every conceivable shape and size are splendidly hung from the ceilings and sides of innumerable small festival stalls. There are usually more than sixty stalls, many of which are fitted out with tatami and charcoal warmers for the merchants' comfort. Crowds mill about, eating, drinking, blowing on fingers, and stamping their feet in the cold. Boisterous sales pitches ring out; the ritual clapping sequence of 3–3–3–1 is heard at each purchase.

Kabuki actors and scenes are the traditional motifs. When I went, the most popular was Tamasaburo. Part of the fun is identifying the actors and the roles in which they are portrayed. A sign of changing times is that many of the younger merchants don't seem to know their Kabuki actors, let alone the famous scenes that their elaborate costumes and poses represent. But I'm sure they have no difficulty in identifying the politicians and cartoon characters found on other, more modern varieties of paddles.

Since the Edo Period, *hagoita* have become increasingly elaborate, until gradually they have taken on a life of their own, quite apart from the game. This year, prices ranged from 850 to a whopping 800,000 yen, but most sales were between 10,000 and 30,000 yen. Certainly most of the *hagoita* sold at the Asakusa festival are too elaborate, too unwieldy, too heavy, and above all too expensive to use for sport. They have become a classic New Year's decoration displayed during December and January.

Hane, or shuttlecocks, range from the plain and emaciated to the frilly and elaborate. Made of soapberry seed and feathers, the different-shaped *hane* made for variously paced games require diverse strategies and techniques. There is no net to worry about; a line is drawn on the ground between the players. The trick is to keep the *hane* in the air, either by repeatedly hitting it by oneself or by hitting it back and forth with an opponent. Much of the fun and style is created by hitting the *hane* straight up to position it for a good whack. The score depends on the number of times the *hane* falls to the ground and is, according to my neighbors, kept by painting *sumi* ink marks on the face of the loser. Sounds a bit messy, but simple? Well . . .

I'm sure the traditional costume was not intended to be an obstacle in itself but, in modern times especially, it can be seen as such. A purist would don a *furisode* kimono (the one with the long sleeves) and thick wooden geta. This is hardly the best outfit for a game involving a fair bit of running. An elaborate hairdo pierced with ornaments and a obi tied tightly around the waist further complicates matters.

If you haven't seen *hanetsuki* played, wander through *shitamachi* during the New Year's holidays. My husband and I hold a grand tournament in my neighborhood every year. We'll have lots of black ink out and some extra *hagoita* as well. But don't forget your long sleeves!

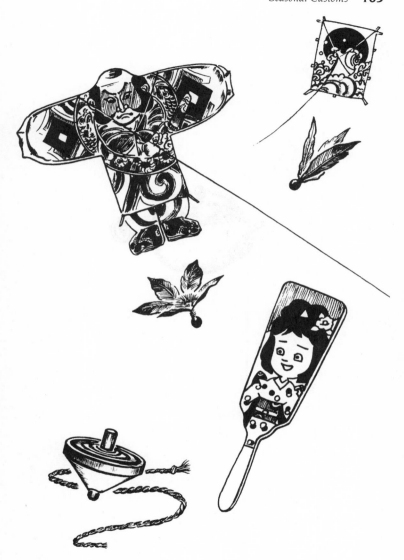

Daily Life

The Public Bath

Perhaps you've wondered why most public baths look like Buddhist temples from the outside. This is a carry-over from the days when temples offered baths to people as a part of their purification rites. Later, in the sixteenth century, public baths as such came into being. They were called *yuya* in the Kanto area and *furoya* in Kansai. The major difference between them, other than their names, was that the Kanto baths were actual baths whereas in the Kansai region they were steam rooms.

Why did people go to the public baths? Private baths were outlawed during the Edo Period (1603–1868) as a fire-prevention measure, so there were no other options. In those days, the public baths opened early in the morning and closed early in the evening. Today, they open around 4:00 P.M. and close near midnight.

If you are searching for a public bath, look for the high, thin chimney that invariably accompanies it. Better look soon, too, as these remnants of an age gone by are vanishing before our eyes.

However, the public baths aren't disappearing as fast as you might think. In 1941 there were 2,792 in Tokyo. As of July 1994, there were 1,669. But the number will decrease rapidly due to the building

boom and the price of land. In my area, several very large baths have been razed to make way for *manshon* condominiums.

The bath in our neighborhood, Majima Yu in Yanaka, is a

beautiful old building built just after the war in traditional style with high ceilings and the usual artistic touches—a large mural of a Fuji-like mountain, and tiled mosaics of Hokkaido scenes along the walls.

One of the things I like best about the public baths is that they are seasonal and have special events. There is the *hana shobu* or iris bath on May 5 to celebrate Boys Day. At this time the baths are filled with iris leaves, and the kids make whistles out of them. During the Obon summer festivals, those who carry the *mikoshi* (portable shrine) get a free pass for a bath. On the winter solstice there is a *yuzu* bath in which the fragrant peels of a special type of Japanese orange that are good for the skin are put into the baths. On these as well as other days, there is the constant gossip and talk of neighbors, something that attracts us all to the place.

The baths have a history of being a community "hot spot." When they became popular in the Edo Period, a second floor was built above the baths where customers could relax, drink tea, eat sweets or sushi, play *igo* or *shogi*, and study *ikebana* (flower arrangement). They were attended by the *yuna*, or women who washed the customers' backs during the day. These women would double as prostitutes and saké servers at night. When two hundred public baths were shut down because of immorality in the 1650s, their *yuna* all went to the famous geisha district, Yoshiwara, to become prostitutes.

In 1885, the baths were separated into male and female sections. Previous to this the dressing rooms had been separate, but the baths themselves were not. Word has it that American missionaries played a large part in the separation. The change was not popular at first, but was gradually effected. Today at most baths there is a tiny Alice-in-Wonderland-type door that connects the men's and women's bathrooms. Children often run between the two.

As Japan is being westernized, more and more young people who have not grown up going to public baths are hesitant about entering them. Because of this, the wonderful system of the *bandai*—the elderly person who collects money from a high perch at the entrance and looks on into both the men's and women's sections and participates in conversations—is being phased out in the new baths. *Bandai* perform an important social function in the community, spreading information and gossip far and wide.

Today's "new baths" (fortunately there aren't many yet) have entrances that eliminate the *bandai*. Despite the inevitable puzzlement on the faces of *bandai* people when I first go to any public bath (foreign customers aren't an everyday occurrence), I like the system and I am sad to see it replaced with an antiseptic hotel-like front desk. If you want to go to a real public bath, you'd better hop in soon.

Bathhouse Art

One of the unsung delights of the public bath, the *sento*, is the hand-painted mural that stretches from the men's bath over a divider into the women's section. A relaxing view of Mount Fuji, Matsushima or some other scenic spot is one of a handful of features that factor into the choice of a bath, along with how close it is to home, how friendly the *bandai* is, and how hot the water is kept.

These huge murals (often 3.6 by 10.8 meters) are painted in a couple of hours. The job requires enormous energy, speed, and a good sense of balance. Toshimitsu Hayakawa, a lively and loquacious artisan, has been working as a *sento* artist for thirty-seven years. He used to knock off two murals a day, about seven hundred a year, but now he says he's down to about three hundred—still an awesome number when you consider that he turns his brushes to billboard painting during the winter. At 40,000 to 50,000 yen a bath, this may be one of the more attractive jobs in Japan: a three- to five-hour workday and no *senpai* (superiors) to hassle you.

Lucrative as this work is, though, its future is tied to the failing public baths. Although there had been about thirty *sento* painters in the fifties when Mr. Hayakawa started, there are now only three, including himself, in the greater Tokyo area. He has had a number of trainees, but all have quit because of the height and precarious balance of the ladders that have to be roped in ingenious ways to prevent sliding on the bath tiles. Even when solidly set up, the painter must "jump" his ladder sideways in order to paint areas beneath it. "I've fallen quite a few times," Mr. Hayakawa admits. "Dislocated arms, bruises, burns. Most often you fall into the bath. Today is the day Tsuru no Yu (Crane Bath) is closed so the baths are empty. But usually a *sento* will open for its afternoon customers right after the job is done. You can get

badly scalded because the water is very hot when the baths are just filled."

Mr. Hayakawa is telling me all of this as he is wielding his brush at a mad pace, high up on his ladder. He's painting blue sky, which fills the top third of the mural. There are more than thirty well-used brushes, each with a specific use, lined up on his scaffolding next to the paint. He plans to execute a huge Mount Fuji over the division between the men's and women's baths so that it towers over both sides. This is an unusual arrangement and the owner of Tsuru no Yu is quite excited.

The oil paint smell is making me dizzy. The bath windows are all thrown open, but it's such a hot, still, muggy day that this does little to displace the fumes. "Doesn't bother me a bit," Mr. Hayakawa claims. "In fact my hobby is oil painting. I have a large repertory for the baths, but I like to paint at least two new scenes a year. In order to do this I travel. You know, some of the murals are of Hawaii ...."

Of this I am aware. And more than 10 percent of the baths have turned to permanent tiled mosaics (often of Hawaiian scenes) that dispense with the hand-painted murals altogether.

The murals are financed through advertising. In the not-so-distant past, of course, just about everyone went to the public baths, which made them an ideal advertising spot. Advertisements were lined up on separate metal plaques under the mural and along the bath itself. As the number of baths continue to diminish and customers are on the wane, advertising has thinned out. Movie posters and local beauty-shop ads are about all that remain. Tokyo's Bunkyo Ward sponsors fourteen murals each year in order to have ward-policy slogans painted on the pictures. For example, there's a cartoon-character hippo on a bicycle with a notice not to abandon your bike at stations; a rabbit on a skateboard with a message promoting less reliance on the Tokyo administration and more responsibility for all wards. Another is a cat invoking owners to take more responsibility for their pets—inspired by the current problem the city is facing with abandoned dogs and cats.

Murals are painted on sheet zinc which lasts years before having to be replaced. If you look closely at the sky of a mural you can see faint traces of former Mount Fuji peaks or palm trees of previous murals (look at places where afternoon light is reflected). At Tsuru no Yu I could pick out three previous mountains on the men's side and one plus a huge palm on the women's. Baths traditionally have their murals repainted once a year, one on top of another. The most unique *sento* mural that I have seen was of a Gauguin Tahitian scene in Asakusa. I was sad to hear that Mr. Hayakawa had painted over that one a little while ago. Although Mr. Hayakawa has painted well over ten thousand murals, in the end he will have nothing to show for it. "Sometimes it discourages me to have to paint over a really good mural, but," he grins, "that's what keeps me in business, isn't it."

Cloth Wrapping

Furoshiki are making a comeback. These decorative cloth wrappers, once the domain of fastidious grandmas, are throwing off their fuddy-duddy image and coming into style. Drop the final "i" of the word *furoshiki*: "furo-chic" is in! But before we delve into the current trend, let's follow the age-worn, multipurpose cloth through the past twelve or thirteen centuries.

The word *furoshiki* was coined in the Edo Period, although the product had been in full use centuries before under the aliases *hira-tsutsumi* and, earlier, *koromo-tsutsumi*. The Shosoin, a Nara Period (710–94) warehouse that holds many important cultural assets of that period, contains some cloth pieces used to wrap Bugaku (court dancing) costumes. There are also pictures depicting women of the mid-Heian Period (794–1185) carrying goods wrapped in cloth on their heads. The banning of private baths (as a fire-prevention measure) and construction of the public baths in the seventeenth century were instrumental in the word change. At the baths people spread out their *hira-tsutsumi* to change their clothes on and afterwards wrapped up their clothes in them. Gradually the *hira-tsutsumi* were renamed *furoshiki* meaning bath (*furo*) and spread out (*shiki*). During the latter part of the Edo Period, with the increase in economic development, *furoshiki* also were more and more commonly used by merchants to carry goods to be sold outside their stores.

Traditionally, most *furoshiki* are purchased as returns for wedding and funeral presents. Today the average household has about eight *furoshiki*. Sales hit their peak in 1972 with 100 million sold. Inexpensive nylon *furoshiki* created this peak, while at the same time cheapening their overall image. This was around the time large stores started providing or selling bags. Sales decreased dramatically and hit a low of 38 million in 1987. But after that, sales of *furoshiki* have picked up a bit and between 40 to 50 million were sold in 1994.

KARAKUSA PATTERN

Ikuzo Tamura of the Miyai Company, the largest *furoshiki* wholesaler in Tokyo, says that the number of *furoshiki* made of natural materials hasn't changed much over the years. Synthetics caused a huge surge in sales, then a decline. But sales of natural fiber *furoshiki* are now about the same as they had been during the peak years. New uses abound: as tablecloths, place settings, and fabric for patchwork quilting and sewing. Sizes range from 45 by 45 centimeters square to bedspread sizes of two meters across; prices run from 500 to 50,000 yen. The Miyai Company also provides a series of modern artists' works and a Boston Museum of Fine Arts Collection of Monet's water lilies. The biggest-selling items are designer *furoshiki* such as those featuring original prints by Hanae Mori and revived traditional patterns of 100-percent cotton or silk.

My favorite pattern, *karakusa*, has an image problem. This and the distinctive *karigane* pattern were developed during the Edo Period. These large bold patterns were distinct from those used by the upper classes. A great deal of what we consider to be "Japanese culture" today came from the *shitamachi* commoners, things like *ukiyoe* woodblock prints, *shamisen* and Kabuki, which were not considered very refined at that time. According to Mr. Tamura, the *karakusa* pattern has recently come to be associated with petty thieves, vagabonds, and people in from the country with heavy loads of vegetables tied to their backs. As in the case of the flared *monpe* pants, an association with the hardship and poverty during and after the Second World War has turned most Japanese off to these unique and beautiful fabric patterns. Sadly, the revival of traditional patterns often involves putting fancy boarders around designs and making the patterns smaller and more Western. I hope this trend will pass and that the bold, attention-getting patterns of the Edo middle class will be revived.

Apart from its new uses, the *furoshiki* is an object whose time has come—or, at any rate, should come. For in this handy age-worn fabric is a solution to a major environmental problem: trash. *Furoshiki* should be taking the place of those ubiquitous plastic bags at grocery stores, paper bags at department stores, and wasteful gift wrapping. Classes on how to wrap things in *furoshiki* should be reinstituted in the schools. *Furoshiki* are environmentally friendly; especially the cotton and silk ones.

Young, fashionable OLs (office ladies) have been wrapping gifts to one another in fancy *furoshiki*—a kind of retro boom considered quite chic. Even Japan's lovely Princess Kiko had her own set of *furoshiki* order-made. If this doesn't start a boom with the younger set, nothing will.

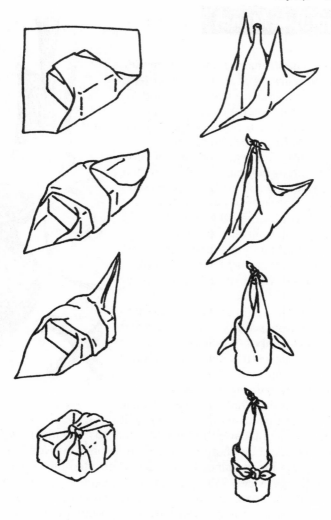

From boxes to bottles, *furoshiki* can be used to wrap nearly any kind of gift.

Tangible Money

Due to chaotic management, my money supply is always depleted, with little to show for it. But we may be moving toward a future where even the stringently frugal will be out of money. Bit by bit, hard, cold cash is becoming less convenient to use. Going are the days of Japanese tourists pulling out rolls from their money belts; going also are the days when housewives pay with bills or coins at the local store. The use of plastic cards, bank transfers, and prepaid services is proliferating. We're in the midst of changes that may land us in a cashless society with no dollars or yen in our pockets.

Over the centuries money has changed from actual goods to paper and coin that symbolize tangible assets, to electrical signals traveling from company to bank to store in intangible form. Today, money in itself (i.e., bills and coins) is inconvertible and has no intrinsic worth, but this wasn't always so. I went to the Bank of Japan's Currency Museum to trace its history and was fascinated by what I learned there. Money evolved from the barter system, and since buyer and seller often didn't want the same things, widely valued commodities came to be used in the exchange. In Japan, two such items were rice and arrowheads. But as rice and sometimes even arrowheads deteriorate with time, coins came into being in the early eighth century.

Modeled after Tang Dynasty coins, the first coins were made of

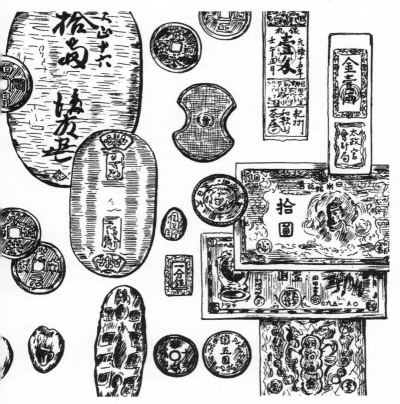

copper and resembled today's five-yen piece, with a square central hole which enabled them to be held still with a square rod while their edges were filed down. Between the twelfth and sixteenth centuries, imported Chinese copper coins were used as the main currency in Japan. When the money supply was insufficient, coins were privately minted, but since the advanced techniques of the Chinese could not be matched, the quality of these home-made coins wasn't good.

It was Toyotomi Hideyoshi who centralized the mintage of gold and silver coins in the sixteenth century. During this time the curious practice of shaving pieces off beautiful gold coins to pay for less expensive objects prevailed. Paper money came into use around 1600, backed by the credit of leading merchants. The New Currency Act created the yen in 1871 and, finally, the Bank of Japan Law ended the yen's convertibility to gold in 1942. From this point on, Japan's money system became a managed one.

Formerly handed over in cash once or twice a month, salaries first began to be transferred to bank accounts (*furikomi*) in the late 1960s, and in fiscal year 1993 (April 1993–March 1994) there were 137 million such transfers. The direct payment of utility bills also circumvented cash transactions through automatic deductions from bank accounts. This started with electricity bills in 1965, followed by water and gas in 1967 and 1968. In 1968 such transfers accounted for less than 10 percent of the electric, water, and gas bills in greater Tokyo. By 1991 these transfers had increased to 80, 70, and 76 percent, respectively. Nowadays, so many services are paid by bank transfers that the act of actually handing over money to pay a bill is becoming rare.

Interesting to note as well is the subtle takeover of some functions that were once the sole domain of banks by non-bank institutions. One such example is NTT's issuing of prepaid cards from which services (phone call charges) are deducted with each use. This represents a substitute form of money that has been issued not by the government, but by a private business. Are banks losing control over money, once their exclusive domain?

The prepaid card is an ingenious coup for the companies issuing them because it allows them to operate on money paid for services not yet rendered. This represents a huge, up-front float, like an interest-free loan. The telephone card, first introduced here in 1982, caught on like wildfire. In fiscal year 1993 alone, 2,613 billion yen was spent for 381 million NTT telephone cards. You may already have experienced the frustration of being unable to find a phone that takes coins.

Cash cards in circulation in Japan went from 51 million cards in 1979 to 284 million cards in March 1994; and credit cards surged from 24 million in 1979 to 215 million in March 1993. And the trend is not limited to adults. A recent survey showed that one in three junior high school students of Setagaya Ward have their own cash cards. It's not surprising that the number of young Japanese being forced into bankruptcy through the misuse of credit is skyrocketing.

Sophisticated real-time or POS (point of sales) cards debit money from bank accounts instantly. Bills are not paid at the end of the month, but at the time of purchase (there goes the bank float between purchase and payment). Fancier cards with their own internal microchips that enable one to check bank balances, buy and sell stocks, and even make airline reservations are currently under development. With all these advances, money as an object is being transformed into electronic signals, no longer represented by coin or paper. Will any of the coins and bills survive the first half of the twenty-first century?

Yusuke Nagamine, head of the Nezu branch of Fuji Bank, is optimistic. "Japanese," he says, "are attached to hand-held cash. No matter how popular cards become, it's more satisfying to use cash on certain occasions. Sure, I use credit cards to buy expensive goods. But for paying for an evening of drinking with friends at a pub? It feels good to pay with cash and get it over with, it's part of the fun of the evening's ritual."

Pawnshops

The origins of the Japanese pawnshop in the form that we know it today go back to the Kamakura Period (1185–1336). But even earlier, during the Nara and Heian periods, temples, government offices, and wealthy people loaned money as a side-business with land used as collateral. Gradually, the collateral changed from land to movable property, and pawnshops built their distinctive, thick-walled warehouses, called *dozo*, to protect the pawned goods. The Edo Period brought great prosperity to the pawn business along with a new name, *shichiya*, which is what they are called today. There were said to be some 2,731 pawnshops in Edo (old Tokyo) alone.

In the present age of charge cards and prosperity, the pawnshop business is in substantial decline. In 1958 there were 21,539 pawnshops in Japan; in 1989, only 6,831 remained. The recorded high in Tokyo was in 1960 with 2,030 shops, but this number shrank to 941 in 1989 and to 780 in June 1994. (Official records go back to 1924.)

Who are the customers? According to Kou Saita, whose family has been in the pawn business for more generations than they have records, at least 60 percent of those pawning things are men, but about 60 percent of those retrieving these goods are women. "Strange, isn't it?" he comments. "But of course, the best things to pawn these days are gold and jewels. It looks like some of my customers have borrowed their wives' jewelry. Especially when not-so-happy wives come to retrieve the goods."

Many of his customers use the pawnshop as a type of family bank. In fact, Mr. Saita has customers whose families have used his shop for three generations. Some may need money suddenly

when banks are closed or may have their cash tied up in stocks or time deposits. Or they are men whose wives keep too tight a purse string. Or politicians. Mr. Saita fulfills an omniscient role of sorts. For ten generations or more his family has been monitoring changes in fashions and has had a front-row view of human drama that makes even a soap opera seem dull.

Before the Second World War, work tools and kimono were typical items to pawn. Today's electrical goods and word processors, because of their short model lifespans, do not command a very high price. At Mr. Saita's establishment camera lenses, precious stones, gold, metal, and stocks and bonds fetch the highest prices. But, he says, the price he pays for the same thing brought in by two different people will differ. Part of his job is to access his customer and how much he values what he pawns.

The payback schedule is set by law. What he can accept is partly set as well. The broker must keep the object for retrieval for a minimum of three months. The charge is 9 percent a month, or 108 percent a year. Legally, cars are out, as well as drugs, alcohol, patents, and land. He doesn't want heirlooms like swords or art. A high percentage of these goods are imitations, and it's a discouraging thing to have to tell a customer the truth.

Mr. Saita's pawnshop is off a narrow alley in the Yanaka area. It is elegant. The entrance is a large wooden gate with a *noren* (an indigo-dyed cloth sign hung like a curtain from the gate or door when a shop is open) leading into a flagstone courtyard that contains a well and lush vegetation. The building is a huge two-story wooden structure built before the Great Earthquake of 1923. It has elegant, heavy tiled roofs and a large, thick-walled warehouse attached. Visually, it conjures up Kyoto. One can imagine a wealthy aristocrat living on such an estate. Even so, my husband Itsuo suggested that our neighbors would have a lot to talk about if anyone saw me going in.

The raunchy image of the pawnshop is largely media-made, Mr. Saita explained. To counteract this he has made snappy telephone cards with the design of his shop's *noren* on them.

Others advertise on TV or in newspapers. It's difficult to learn the trade, and the things being pawned are changing so fast that the broker has to be knowledgeable in all fields. In order to be successful, he has to be somewhat of a scholar. And he must be able to make decisions instantly. There is a pawnbrokers' association that helps them adapt to the quick pace of today's changes, introducing them to the latest technologies, and warning them of what fakes are going around. They hold a study meeting once a month.

This place could turn out useful, I thought. Being an artist's wife and having had many occasions when the rent could not be paid on time, I was momentarily intrigued. Until I realized that we don't have anything we could pawn. No gold, no diamonds, no camera lenses. Not even an engagement ring!

Japanese Inns

Traveling was a necessity for officials of seventh-century Japan, and the government instituted a "station system" that required the wealthy to feed and put them up. Other travelers, however, had to sleep in temples or outdoors. It wasn't until around the tenth century that ryokan, or inns, came into use. Their number increased over the following centuries due to religious pilgrimages, merchants peddling their wares, and others looking for work. By the Edo Period (1603–1868) numerous inns were located along main roads like the Tokaido, which extended from Kyoto to Edo (old Tokyo). Traveling in those days was a dusty, often dangerous ordeal, but the wives and children of powerful lords were forced to spend alternate years in Edo by the Tokugawa government as an assurance of loyalty. This government set up rigid regulations for inns and check stations, and various types of ryokan developed to accommodate different classes of people.

The most comfortable inns were the *honjin*, for court nobility and local lords. A combination of samurai residence and inn, these were constructed to both be strong enough to protect guests from their enemies and provide a choice of emergency exits. H*atagoya* were inns for ordinary travelers. Their employees pulled in customers from off the street. Once caught, the guest was presented with a basin of hot water by a young waitress, with which to wash his feet. After this he received tea, took a bath, and had dinner in his room. At some point the owner would appear to ascertain whether the guest was "suspicious" or not. If so, this was reported to the authorities. Prostitution was an attraction at many of these inns, as it had been right along. By the mid-nineteenth century, competition was tough: thirty-four of the fifty-three stations along the Tokaido had inns that provided prostitutes for their customers.

Cheaper inns called *shonin yado* were available for merchants. For the lowest class, there was the *kichin yado* which offered only

bedding plus wood, for an extra fee, with which to cook one's own meals.

Many general ryokan were still in operation after the Second World War, but the numbers have shrunk drastically with the postwar prosperity. The Sawa family has been running a twelve-room ryokan in Tokyo since 1949. Isao Sawa explained that customers had been dropping off until at one point in 1982 he had no customers at all. Originally catering to school travel groups, tourists, and businessmen, Mr. Sawa's inn provides warm, personal service. One day he prepares flowers for a wedding couple's room; the next he throws them out, and takes the phone and TV out of the room in preparation for a large group of students.

"Japanese have changed," he says. "When I was growing up there were lots of kids, housing was cramped, and we all slept in one room. Nowadays, students and businessmen use hotels because they can't sleep with their friends in the same room. The advantage of tatami is that it makes a room expandable. Until recently many businesses had overnight office parties where everyone ate and slept in one or two huge rooms. Another change is that businessmen want to go out at night, so they don't like our 11:00 P.M. curfew."

Mr. Sawa had to change or go out of business. With great trepidation he joined the Japanese Inn Group, a group of seventy-five inns welcoming non-Japanese guests, and opened his ryokan to foreigners. In 1993 he had 6,100 visitors from fifty countries. They are booked solid. He laughs when he talks about it: "Japanese take short trips, see famous sights, and stay in lavish Western-style hotels. The luxury hotel is one focus of the travel. We want to get away, even if just mentally, and we don't want to be reminded of home by tatami or Japanese-style baths. Foreigners are different. They travel for long periods of time and use their money for things other than accommodation. And they take so much pleasure in seeing an old neighborhood like this."

In between greeting guests and answering the phone, Mr. Sawa told me that regular ryokan don't have a future. And even those that accept foreign guests like his will not survive forever in places with high land prices like Tokyo. "The inheritance tax is too high. We don't make much profit so we can't save up for it." But he smiles with real pride about the many visitors who come back year after year to his inn. He had started with little English and no knowledge of foreign customs. After only twelve years he is a prominent figure in the field of ryokan for non-Japanese.

Sawanoya and the other establishments in the Japanese Inn Group, which was founded in 1979, are not just a cheap place to stay (4,000 to 5,000 yen per night), they are an experience. Taking a Japanese bath and sleeping in traditional bedding on tatami is delightful. Besides this, there is a chance to get to know the family and surrounding neighborhood. It's an extraordinary way to see Japan.

Repairs

In Japan almost everyone owns the latest consumer goods. The worth of antiques hasn't hit the mainstream yet and few people purchase anything secondhand. As in the past, customers are fussy about their purchases and poorly designed goods rarely clutter the market. The difference today lies in the slew of non-biodegradable goods coupled with profligate spending. "In the past," says Kazuko Iiyama, a second-generation futon repairer, "possessions were few and special."

Japan is now at war with an insurmountable heap of trash. Tokyo alone is going from tossing 13,427 tons per day in 1989 and 14,683 tons per day in 1992 to a predicted 17,649 tons a day in the year 2000. Inventive measures have been taken to swallow the mess, resulting in various creations from a landfill in Tokyo Bay called "Dream Island" to a low-rate golf course with pipes hidden behind bushes to allow the escape of methane gas, the product of decomposing elements beneath. The latter is the first non-smoking golf course in Japan (if not the world), having been made so to prevent explosions. Where the trash of today will end up tomorrow is anyone's guess.

"Even if we can afford it, the way we live now is a terrible waste," continues Mrs. Iiyama. She is sitting properly on her legs leaning against more than fifty bolts of gaily colored fabrics which are wedged in among neatly packed parcels of cotton. For forty-one years she has been busy making, cleaning, and restuffing traditional bedding. There used to be much more work. People kept extra futon in their closets for when relatives visited. With today's convenient transportation system and the

availability of hotels, relatives either return to the country or stay in a hotel. She thinks the change is also partly due to "*manshon* life" in the new condominium apartments. There is less space to store extra futon, making it difficult to have them restuffed at all. Another cause is the emergence of synthetic fibers. A futon with less than 40-percent cotton stuffing cannot be cleaned and restuffed. Thus, many people, particularly singles, buy the cheaper synthetic futon and throw them out when they move or when the bedding needs cleaning. Even customers who have the cotton-stuffing variety and used to have them cleaned every two years, now make do with restuffing once every five years or more.

The shoe repair business is also getting a cramp. Tokyo's 1,909 shoemakers in 1956 were worn down to 683 by July 1994. There are now only five or six shoemakers in the whole of Bunkyo Ward. One of them, Seiji Tamura, shoemaker and repairer for sixty-six years, once made about seventy pairs of shoes a month. Today he makes few shoes and fixes even fewer. Of course the fast, convenient Mr. Minit shoe repairs are available. But Mr. Tamura believes that ready-made shoes may not be worth repairing and that customers that know about shoes, especially those who wear order-made ones, are careful to have them properly repaired at the right time.

"The way shoes are mass produced these days is no damn good. I can tell by the way people walk whether their shoes fit correctly—most don't," he clears his throat. "It's because shoes are so bad these days that sneakers have become so popular." He adds cocking his head, "Great sneakers, though . . . "

Bicycle repairs are also off-course, says Yoshinobu Nagao, repairer for thirty-eight years. "Now that bicycles are so cheap, instead of fixing them, people abandon them on the street or at subway stations and buy new ones." The number of bicycle repairers in Tokyo has gone from about 3,700 in 1950 to 2,089 in 1994. It's decreasing rapidly because there aren't any successors. "Flat tires and brake and chain repairs are my most frequent work, but the future's in selling new, expensive bikes," he says pointing to a row of gleaming off-road and racing cycles. "I still do 'after-care,' but there's less and less of it." As he says this and shakes his head, a group of schoolboys screech to a stop and clatter in through the sliding door; a flat tire.

The general fix-it-all, or *benriya*, is an endangered species. Electronic goods are all but impossible to get repaired, and even when a repairman can be found, it's usually cheaper to buy a new product. The sales point of many new products is that they are disposable, like the one-use razors, disposable cameras, and 500-yen plastic umbrellas. Instead of bothering with the maintenance of a house, the solution is often to rebuild it entirely. This trend is compounded by industry-friendly built-in obsolescence. If last year's new sink has a leak and you are lucky enough to find a plumber who has time to fix it, chances are that you will be told that the entire bathroom plumbing needs to be replaced with newer, more up-to-date materials.

These days about the only repair work that seems to be booming is that done by doctors on our own biodegradable, but indispensable parts!

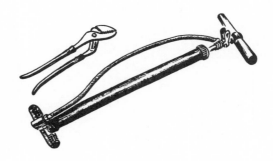

Entertainment

Geisha

The original geisha were men skilled in the military arts. Later, the all-male Kabuki actors were sometimes referred to by this word, but it wasn't until the Genbun Era (late 1730s) that "geisha" came to mean entertainers, both male and female.

Strictly speaking, from the mid-eighteenth century, the word "geisha" designated only those skilled in the art of *shamisen*, dance, song, and conversation who worked at the famous Yoshiwara brothels. They were quite separate from the courtesans who plied their more carnal trade after the geisha finished their early evening entertainment. Geisha types outside of the Yoshiwara were called *shaku-onna* or *machi-geisha*, and those from the Fukagawa district made up the second main group in Edo (old Tokyo). Gradually people started using the word "geisha" to refer to them as well, although the real geisha of the Yoshiwara were quite distinct. The Kansai version of the geisha was called by another name, *"geiko."*

The real geisha spent his or her days at lessons, studying the traditional Japanese arts. For a time, the Yoshiwara was a true center of culture, attracting students of dance and music during the days as well as evening customers. Even today, work as a geisha offers a Japanese woman the rare opportunity of a well-paid career that can be pursued to an advanced age. Some quit and open expensive restaurants called *ryotei*; others marry wealthy and powerful men, but many continue on as geisha well into their seventies. Geisha have long had a considerable connection with politics. The samurai involved in the Meiji Restoration (1868) made their plans in Kyoto teahouses. Today, the different government factions also enjoy geisha during behind-the-scenes negotiations at *ryotei*. Akasaka, connected with Japan's ruling parties, has become one main center for geisha.

Geisha are organized into groups in *hanamachi*, or flower towns, centered around registry offices called *kenban*. These organize and coordinate the schedules of all geisha within their district for entertainment, which is provided only at designated *ryotei*. After a party breaks up, a geisha may be taken along to other parties, but is required to keep her *kenban* informed so she can be called to other *ryotei*. The system is still strongly in place. When I went to have an interview with an Asakusa geisha, it was scheduled by the *kenban*.

"Taro-nesan," as she is called, is a geisha from the Asakusa district. Her name, Taro, is a hint that she started her career before the Second World War, when geisha—for practical reasons on the customer's side—were often called men's names, a custom which fell off after the war. With quick and graceful movements, Taro-nesan, dressed in a snappy, patterned kimono with an obi deco-

rated with wisteria, ushered me into a huge tatami room. She had her hair done up; her makeup was soft and natural looking. Before she spoke I was impressed by her presence alone. She has elegance, but without a trace of pride or distance. My expectations of what a geisha should be were reconfirmed by her intelligence, humor, intimacy, and ineffable charm: here is the real thing, the pure geisha.

Taro-nesan's start in the geisha world had none of the tragedy of a family selling a child to pay the bills. She lived near the Asakusa *kenban* and had longed to become a geisha. Her dance and *shamisen* lessons started at the age of ten. "I thought of nothing but walking about on those high *pokkuri* geta wearing luxurious kimono with my hair piled up in a fancy style; I had no idea of how challenging a geisha's life would be. I entered the *okiya* (geisha house) at fourteen and became a full-fledged geisha when I was twenty years old. I had to live in the *okiya* during those six years, but afterwards I moved back with my mother."

She ranks at the top of the *shamisen* world, a fact attested to by walls of certificates. Although she makes occasional performances at places like the National Theater, she spends most afternoons teaching accomplished students. When asked how her work as a geisha has changed, she commented, "Customers have changed. They used to come as individuals, pay with their own money. Those customers truly loved traditional arts and knew how to enjoy an evening with geisha. Salarymen make terrible customers. They come in groups and their company pays. Most don't understand song, dance, music, or intelligent conversation. They don't know how to enjoy themselves in the traditional, elegant ways. I do less work now because these customers want to do the singing themselves: we listen to their *karaoke*. I miss the refined, easygoing men of the past. The Kabuki actors' schedules are too busy now and they no longer have patrons that take them to us . . . "

There was even a politician whose brief career as prime minister ended abruptly some years ago due to a geisha problem prompted by his lack of manners. It's a sad fact that the geisha system depends on men who are educated, refined, and cultured—as well as rich. It is on this point that its foundations are shaking.

Taro-nesan's *kenban* has four new geisha, ages 18, 19, 20, and 25, but numbers are declining. Before the war her area in Asakusa had about 1,300 geisha, in 1957 the number was about 500, and today there are 75 female and 5 male geisha who work at eighteen *ryotei*. Most of them are quite advanced in age, although, as with Taro-nesan at seventy-five, their customers may not know just how much!

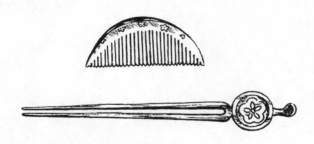

Kabuki Applause

The Japanese have refined shouting to the level of an art; get a ticket for any Kabuki performance and listen. Verbal cacophony

hurtles down from the balconies in loud, staccato shouts, like the clamor of New Yorkers hailing taxi cabs. But, despite the volume, these are the cries of true sophisticates, Kabuki *tsu* (experts) who pride themselves on their knowledge of traditional art.

A few months ago I met Susumu Hirabayashi at the Kabukiza. He was sitting next to me, eyes tightly closed, and appeared to be catching up on his sleep until an ear-splitting "Kinokuniya!" erupted from his lips.

"Kinokuniya" is the *yago*, or acting-house name, of Sawamura Tanosuke, a talented actor of female roles. And Mr. Hirabayashi, high in the balcony, is one of the Kabuki aficionados who call out these *yago*, or an actor's generation number, in appreciation of an

adept pose or performance. The shouts are called *kakegoe*, the shouters *omuko* after the "great beyond" of the back balcony where they once made their calls.

"The real trick," says Mr. Hirabayashi, "is timing. You have to catch a pause in the dialogue, so you have to know the dialogue well. Each actor has his own pace, so what may be an appropriate pause for one may not be for another. I learned through listening. Certain parts just stick in your mind and over the years, through experience, you come to know where to call out."

On his first trip to Kabuki, at the age of sixteen, he saw *Chushingura* and was hooked. Since then, he has shouted out *kakegoe* at two or three performances every month for forty-four years. Several *kakegoe* groups have free passes to Kabuki theaters, and many of these *omuko* are on the payroll of the actors whose names they call out. According to one actor, the art of *kakegoe* has gone down over the past thirty years because of the "semi-pro" nature of many of them. But Mr. Hirabayashi is a loner, buying his own ticket, calling out for free, out of pure love.

Usually he sits in the third balcony. He prefers the right side as he faces the stage so he can see the *hanamichi*, a projection of the stage that passes through the audience on which actors make flashy entrances and exits. What to others may seem a remote seat carries for an *omuko* real pride and status. Calling out from the first floor is bad manners.

"To understand us I guess you have to be familiar with the customs of the Edo Period (1603–1868). This was a time of rigid hierarchy with samurai at the top followed by farmers, laborers, and merchants at the bottom. Samurai attended Noh and Kyogen theater in a refined manner. Kabuki, theater for the commoners, where communication between the actors and their audience was important, was quite different. Ranked even lower than the commoners, actors were not allowed surnames and the *yago*, which developed at the end of the seventeenth century, came from their desire for something more than a first name.

"Screaming out *daikon* (radish) at a poor performer or *hyakusho* (farmer) at an *omuko* who fluffs his call was part of the fun atmosphere of a theater. The *yago*, an actor's generational number; *daitoryo* (president); or *mattemashita* (we've been waiting for this) are the usual calls today. There aren't many who know when and how to call out 'farmer' at one who flubs his timing. And since about ten years ago, a few women's voices have been heard," he adds uneasily.

According to Mr. Hirabayashi, the audience has changed—lots of young people and the third balcony is almost always packed with foreigners. This foreign interest doesn't surprise him. As he puts it, "How else can they learn to understand Japan? Modern high-tech doesn't tell you much, but Kabuki reflects the Japanese way of thinking simply, without much artifice. The sad part of the current Kabuki boom is that on some days there are almost no *kakegoe* heard because the third balcony is occupied by tour groups."

Communication between actors and their audience remains important in Kabuki. Both the skillful calling of *yago* and the clapping of the regular audience help nurture good actors. Sawamura Tanosuke, an important actor from a three-hundred-year line, says that hearing his *yago* called out with the appropriate timing inspires and invigorates him. If called out in a strange place, however, the *kakegoe* can be a real nuisance and throw him off.

Mr. Hirabayashi knows the words of most scripts by heart. He even sounds like a Kabuki actor when he recites them. The future of *kakegoe* may be secure thanks to the members of the *kakegoe* groups who have free access to the theaters, but men like Mr. Hirabayashi, men of taste and culture, who hold broad, deep interest in the arts, are a truly vanishing breed. Japan's transformation from a poor country, rich in cultural tastes, to a rich country with less impressive pastimes holds a sad, strange irony.

TANOSUKE FAMILY CREST

Shinto Juggling

Vaudeville has enjoyed a long and popular history in this country, but with recent social refinements, it and other remnants of Japan's bygone entertainment are being swept away. The problem lies partly in the many new, competing forms of enjoyment and partly in the perception that vaudeville is just plain unsophisticated. Further adding to the problem, vaudeville theaters are being torn down one after another.

The center focus of Japanese vaudeville is traditional storytelling called *rakugo*. Between *rakugo* performances, for a change of pace, special juggling and balance acts called *daikagura* are performed. Whereas *rakugo* has successfully transplanted itself to TV (though its once-sophisticated humor has been reduced to raunchiness), *daikagura* is another story. If you don't see it soon, you may never again have a chance.

Performances include amazing feats of balance along with baton, knife, and hat juggling. *Dontsuku*, acrobatics done with an intricate wicker basket and balls, is perhaps the best-known because it became so popular in the nineteenth century that it was integrated into many Kabuki performances. Also there is *dobin*, the balancing of earthen pots on a stick, and *gokaijawan*, five tiers of teacups and wooden boards balanced on top of a long wooden stick. And many more.

Daikagura's roots stretch back to the eighth century's street performances (*daidogei*). It started as sacred music and dance for the Shinto religion, with a *shishi* dance that was performed with a giant lion's head. This purification ritual took place at the entrances of prosperous homes at New Year's and was also provided for people who were too ill or frail to visit their shrine. Gradually it came to be accompanied with acrobatics and comical plays, and by the Edo Period there were thirteen different types of *daikagura* performances. Although Kabuki actors of the day were looked down upon, performers of *daikagura* were given the unusual honor of maintaining a family name and wearing swords, both of which were denied to commoners.

Of the two main streams of *daikagura*, originating at the Ise Shrine in Mie Prefecture and at the Atsuta Shrine in Aichi, the Atsuta Shrine performers were first to travel to Edo (in 1664) to perform for wealthy households. Instantly popular, they were

summoned to perform for the shogun in 1669. After this they visited Edo every year to do the lion dance and lead festival processions (at Hie Jinja and Kanda Myojin). They eventually organized twelve groups in Edo. Not to be outdone, in 1674 the Ise school also moved to Edo and organized its own twelve groups. The competing groups were finally harmonized in 1817 when they met and made rules to govern their activities.

Today there are about twenty *daikagura* performers, only four or five of whom perform in traditional fashion. Senjuro Kagami, a thirteenth-generation artist, is one of them. Adopted into the twelfth Kagami household as an apprentice at the age of eight, his rigorous training included two hours of practice before he went to school (starting at 5:00 A.M.) and another two hours or more before dinner. He was forced to juggle batons 100 consecutive times without making a mistake before he was allowed to eat dinner. It was not an enjoyable childhood. After two years of practice, Senjuro made his debut at a local vaudeville theater. Only ten years old, he was terrified, but not as much, he says, as when he performed in front of Emperor Hirohito several years later. He disgraced himself by dropping a plate he was juggling, but Prince Takamatsu, the Emperor's brother, saved the day. He told Senjuro not to worry, that if he hadn't made the mistake, the Emperor "would have become uneasy thinking that Senjuro was so perfect that he must be a god."

Today Senjuro's schedule includes at least 300 performances a year including 120 to 130 at elementary schools. Things are more difficult than they used to be because he is expected to talk to the audience while he is performing. Customer reaction is important and he claims that foreigners are his best audience. "Japanese," he says, "are burnt out. They don't know how to look anymore. Watching so much television has made them passive. Former audiences were lively and hard to please, but nowadays, most Japanese just watch with a blank face."

His performances, done in formal kimono and *hakama* (a pleated skirt worn over kimono), are executed with charisma and panache.

LION DANCE

Most impressive for me were the long wooden batons he balanced on his face. He could transfer a ball from the top of one to the other without using his hands. Impressive also were objects rolled on top of a traditional umbrella. In succession a ceramic teacup, a metal ring, and a *masu* (a square wooden box used as a measure) clattered over the bamboo spokes of the umbrella with a delightful sound that left me breathless . . . and wondering how on earth he did it!

Old Toys

Water pistols, paper balls, noise balloons, *take tonbo* (bamboo flyers), elephants' trunks, cut-out paper doll clothes, glittering stickers, and firecrackers are piled in orderly heaps on top of each other in wood-rimmed glass boxes. Huge glass jars bulge with red fireballs, bubble gum, and chocolate animals. The room has the darkness of age-stained wood from which a kaleidoscope of colors, a waterfall of trinkets, gadgets, and sweets beckon in gaudy seduction. One's attention lurches from jumping frogs and wooden snakes to miniature yen, lollipops, and glorious streamers; one is tempted to reach out and touch the shimmering array, to crinkle the rose- and blue-colored cellophane wrappings.

In the back of the shop there is a step up to a six-mat tatami room where Fuji Kimura and her middle-aged daughter sit, stuffing trinkets into plastic wrappers and drinking tea. Their legs are tucked under a *kotatsu* blanket, warm under the low table heater, and from their perch they look out through the penny-candy store clear to the other side of the street where a dog has backed a snarling cat up against a wooden fence. Although it's a chilly 11:00 A.M., the doors are thrown open and the glittery brightness of the wrappings and plastics twinkles out at the occasional passerby.

The two of them have sat like this for the past forty years, watching children grow up and the neighborhood change. These days, it is not unusual for former customers to visit with their own children or grandchildren in tow, kids who act as if they'd be more comfortable flipping through computer game stacks, confused

perhaps at the panorama of cheap goods. But the parents dart here and there, recalling simple, joyous days when five yen could buy them a handful of sweets or a mechanical trinket or two that would occupy them and their friends for hours.

Even today, 60 yen will buy you a pocketful. According to Mrs. Kimura, the current bestsellers are mostly between 10 and 30 yen. For just 10 yen you can sink your teeth into a fluffy shortbread cake, or try a skewer of apricot sweets. Sixty yen will buy you a shiny multicolored jump-rope, a water pistol, a heli-propeller, or a nose-glasses-mustache disguise. The most expensive items are set between 300 to 500 yen and don't sell so well. Asked whether children have changed in the last forty years, Mrs. Kimura pauses, looks down at a thin silver ring on her right hand, pats her hairnet with the other, and thinks for several minutes. "You know, they *have* changed. They used to come running in here, calling out to me, and we used to talk. You know, I'd ask them about school or their brother or something and the kids used to respond, enthusiastically. If asked, they would sing me a song. They were excited and they would ask me what they should buy. Nowadays, the kids have one hand in their mother's and with the other they paw around. They are picky about what they buy. I think the schools make them finicky like this. And no matter what I ask them, they almost never answer. They don't really talk anymore—they act shy, I suppose. But I don't really think that it's being shy. Strange, isn't it."

By this time I am blowing on my fingers. My hands are cold. I ask the two if they want a modern building, one that might be a bit warmer. Mrs. Kimura seems reluctant to answer my question, as if ashamed to give me the wrong answer. "Frankly," she says, "I like the cold. I like the cracks and drafts in this old house. And I always leave the store door open, even in the winter. Maybe it's because I'm in my seventies, but I like a direct connection with the outdoors. Take the new building next door. It may have the same dust as we have here, but in an old house dust has a mood. In a *manshon* (condominium apartment), it doesn't. They've got the same air, but it feels different. They're completely cut off from the outside, from people, from nature. No, I don't want a new home, I just want to continue with my toy business, as I always have."

Index
of Japanese Terms

amado, rain shutters, 44, 143
amezaiku, candy art, 18

bandai, proprietor's seat at public
    bath, 169
benriya, general repairman, 193
bon odori, summer festival
    dancing, 130

chindonya, publicity band, 15
chonai-kai, neighborhood
    association group, 108, 132

dagashiya, seller of traditional
    toys and candy, 208
daikagura, Shinto juggling, 204
daimei nosatsu, a type of *senja fuda*,
    96
dezomeshiki, New Year's balancing
    act performed by the fire
    brigade, 68

ema, votive plaque, 116
Edo sashimono, woodwork with
    fancy joinery, 84

furikomi, bank transfers, 180
furoshiki, wrapping cloth, 157, 174

futon, bedding, 190

geisha, professional entertainers,
    196
genkin, cash, 178
geta, clogs, 64, 128, 140, 162

hachimaki, headband, 20
hanami, flower viewing (esp.
    cherry blossoms), 122
hanetsuki, Japanese-style
    battledore, 160
haragake, artisan's apron with
    pouches (also called *donburi*),
    20, 128
hatsuyume, first dream of the year,
    156
heri, decorative fabric boarder of
    tatami, 40
hikeshi, fire fighters, 70
"*hi no yojin*", "beware of fires", 71,
    150
hyogushi, paper mounter, 104
hyoshigi, wooden clappers, 22, 71,
    150

iki, refined Japanese elegance,
    86, 101

jishinban, patrolling system during the Edo period, 150

jubako, lacquer boxes for *osechi ryori*, 152

Kabuki, Japanese classical drama, 78, 200

kakejiku, hanging scroll, 104

kakegoe, shouts of appreciation by Kabuki fans, 201

kakigori, crushed ice, 142, 144

kamishibai, paper picture theater, 22

katorisenko, mosquito repellant, 140

kawara, tile roof, 52

kaya, mosquito netting, 142

kayabuki yane, thatched roof, 56

kenban, geisha registry office, 196

kijishi, wood lather, 72

kiseru, long pipe, 30

kizami, chopped tobacco for *kiseru*, 32

kokan nosatsu, a type of *senja fuda*, 100

kumade, an ornamental rake, 134

maiko, young traditional dancer of Kyoto, 66

meotobake, special brushes used to apply *senja fuda*, 98

mikoshi, portable shrine, 88, 168

miyashi, portable-shrine artisan, 88

mon, family crest, 42

nagaya, long wooden apartments, 59, 148

ninjo, warm human relations, 60

nokigake, short *sudare*, 50

Obon, Buddhist festival of the dead, 168

omote, (*tatami omote*) surface of tatami, 40

onigawara, demon roof-tiles, 54

oreiboko, artisan's working without pay to thank master, 91

osechi ryori, New Years' cuisine, 152

oyakata, boss or teacher of a group of workers, 16, 28, 86

ramen, Chinese noodles, 26

ranma, a carved wooden transom between rooms, 45

raoya, cleaner and fitter of *kiseru* pipes, 30

ryokan, Japanese inn, 186

senja fuda, name stickers for temple and shrine pilgrimages, 96

sento, public bath, 166, 170

shichifukujin, the seven lucky gods, 28, 156

shichiya, pawn shop, 182

shitamachi, old section of Tokyo, 28, 59, 111, 130, 137, 150

shoji, paper sliding screens or doors, 44, 114

sudare, bamboo blinds, 48, 142

takarabune, treasure ship, 156

tatami, floor matting, 40, 188

tatamiya, maker of floor matting, 40

tateguya, interior woodworker, 44

tennengori, ice made naturally
    outdoors, 144
tenugui, cotton handcloth, 80
tobishoku, local construction
    worker, 69, 108
toko, base of tatami, 40
tokonoma, wall niche for display of
    art or flowers, 42

ukiyoe, a type of woodblock print,
    92, 104

wagasa, Japanese umbrella, 76
washi, handmade paper, 78, 107,
    113

yago, acting-house name of
    Kabuki actors, 201
yakiimo, baked sweet potatoes, 28
yukata, informal cotton kimono,
    80, 129, 130, 142

zori, straw footwear, 57, 66